DISCARD

19340

McCOOK COMMUNITY COLLEGE
Learning Resource Center

DATE DUE

staff			
MY 6 '86			
NOV 1 2 '98			
	DISCARD		

GAYLORD | | | PRINTED IN U.S.A.

UCATION

D1247460

Music and Art in Elementary Education

(inner-city edition)

Marvin S. Adler
*Jackie Robinson Intermediate
School of Brooklyn*

George E. Szekely
*Richmond College of the City
University of New York*

A DOCTORATE ASSOCIATION
OF NEW YORK EDUCATORS SERIES

KENDALL/HUNT PUBLISHING COMPANY
Dubuque, Iowa

DISCARD
M_____ COMMUNITY COLLEGE
Learning Resource Center

19340

Copyright © 1976 by Marvin S. Adler and George E. Szekely

Library of Congress Catalog Card Number: 75—44896

ISBN 0—8403—1394—2

All rights reserved. No part of this publication may be reproduced,
stored in a retrieval system, or transmitted, in any form or by any
means, electronic, mechanical, photocopying, recording, or otherwise,
without the prior written permission of the copyright owner.

Printed in the United States of America

contents

foreword

PART ONE

The beauty of this text is that it is so concise for the amount of material covered. At the same time it is detailed enough for the classroom teacher to comprehend the concepts and musical examples without becoming confused. We have here both an introduction to music and a reference for the classroom teacher who is interested in becoming a music specialist. A substantial amount of material has been provided as a basic background upon which the teacher can build and then go beyond the contents of this book to expand his or her knowledge of music.

A faulty and very common practice is avoided—that of taking one or two musical examples and showing how one can teach many concepts. Instead, the teacher's mind is opened to the wealth of material that is available for classroom use (from classical to popular, folk, rock, or jazz). Also, the assumption is not made that every classroom teacher has a good background in music history. All periods in music history are discussed, and appropriate literature selected from each one. Without becoming overly pedantic, the author succinctly states the pertinent ideas that one should know in order to become an effective teacher of music.

Upon completion of this material, the classroom teacher should: (1) have a good working knowledge of musical notation and musical terms; (2) be able to organize a music lesson without having to refer to this book for minor details; (3) have an excellent chronological background of important facts in music history; and (4) understand specific urban problems.

Dr. Jesse C. McCarroll
New York City Community College

PART TWO

Art Education at present needs a strong central concept. This text reestablishes art itself as the primary concern of art education. The artist is presented as a model and guide for art teaching, and the work of contemporary artists as the principle resource of the art program.

This book, written by the painter George Szekely, brings to it all the sensitivities, insights, and innovations of the creator concerned with the education of the future artist. Although illustrated by children's artwork, there are no simple recipes or instantaneous solutions offered to the teacher. This book represents a guide to the study of the artist and suggestions to becoming the artist-teacher. It compares art teaching to art working in which the creative act must be shaped by the individual practitioner. The art teacher is asked to thoughtfully participate in applying the learnings from this book to program planning and innovation.

The urban art program as described by Dr. Szekely is based on the experience of the city and its designers—the visual artists. Art education must involve itself with the fine arts, the popular arts, and the electronic media. The popular arts represent a natural outgrowth of children's extracurricular interests and awarenesses of the streets and environment outside the school.

The arguments presented illuminate the difficulties of the art program in the school with a predominant verbal emphasis. Since art is a form of visual expression and communication, the teacher of art is urged to rely on visual communicative skills in the teaching of art.

The use of contemporary art as a base for elementary art education is a unique proposal in helping students meet the continuous challenges of the rapidly changing art world. *This text focuses on urban educational issues* seldom touched upon by art education; the art education of the non-English speaking child who is usually excluded from art learning before mastering verbal language and the career education of the artist. The art teacher is urged to view the class not as potential consumers or appreciators of art but as artists whose early block playing and paper cutting form the fundamental understandings for the future artist.

Dr. Edith DiChiara
Herbert H. Lehman College
of the City University of
New York

preface

This book includes a practical approach to teaching art and music in inner-city elementary schools, as well as a theoretical base. It is intended for students who plan to be classroom teachers and who do not have an extensive background in music and art. It also can be used by music or art majors who intend to go into teaching. While the authors assume that students have no art or music training, art or music majors can use this text to learn an approach to teaching in urban elementary schools. Nonmusic or art majors can learn an approach to dealing with a city environment as well as teaching fundamentals. The text can be a complete course in itself or be used in conjunction with other books dealing with methods of approaching classroom art and music in elementary schools.

Without the help of the following people, this book would not have been possible, and sincere appreciation is expressed to Dr. Jesse McCarroll, Laura Szekely, and Muriel Adler for proofreading and making many valuable suggestions; to Harris Romaner and Herbert Bender for photography and artwork; to Mark Adler for photography, developing, and printing all photographic material; to Bernard Bricker and Richard Bomer for musical assistance; to Robert Kirin for ideas on presenting music lessons; to Ronald Pencrazi for design assistance; and to James Turner and Thomas Gannon for advice on aspects of special education. We are indebted to the Rhythm Band Incorporated and other manufacturers of instruments mentioned herein, as well as the facilities of the Jackie Robinson Intermediate School 320 of Brooklyn (Adele Charyn, Principal).

Marvin S. Adler
George Szekely

introduction

Art and music are everywhere. Yet traditional approaches in elementary school have made them seem divorced from the art and music we both see and hear around us. We think of school art as finger painting, tracing animals, coloring books, and white paste. We think of school music as singing patriotic songs and playing rhythm instruments—possibly the staging of a musical play. Both can be **so** much more.

The purpose of this book is to open new horizons—to make the prospective (or beginning) classroom teacher realize and employ the diverse multitude of artistic possibilities.

Every time we open a magazine we see: (1) photographs; (2) cartooning; (3) lettering; (4) layouts and design; (5) artistic staging of pots and pans or foods; (6) creative packaging of foods **plus the artwork on the packages of food;** (7) aesthetic design of cars and furniture; and (8) pictures of and reference to the architectural designs (buildings, bridges, aquaducts, and tunnels) that are all around us.

Every time we go to the movies or turn on the radio or television we hear: (1) musical commercials; (2) unique musical themes for specific programs; (3) movie background that creates moods of suspense or excitement; (4) an incredibly wide assortment of popular jazz, folk, or classical music that includes rock, soul, and Hispanic styles; (5) station identification musical themes; and (6) experimental use of electronic sounds.

The special contribution of this book is **not** to synthesize the relationship of art and music—both are individual disciplines. (When we open the magazine we don't hear music; when we turn on the radio we don't see visual arts.) Knowing that there is a relationship between the music of Palestrina and the painting of Leonardo DaVinci will not necessarily enable the child to employ a natural awareness of the art and music everywhere around us. The special contribution of this book is to update the diverse possibilities for art and music in elementary schools.

This book can be used in both music or art method courses—as well as a general elementary methods course. The philosophical issues of "play" and "the artist as a model" have enormous import for music teaching. When reading Part Two (Art) of this book, many musical possibilities both grow and emerge from the ideas presented. Music lessons can be based upon using musical performers as "models" of instruction. Similarly, when reading Part One (particularly Chapter Three *Toward Becoming A Music Specialist*), a prospective classroom teacher can get many ideas for becoming an art specialist and/or using art in a school: (1) for making scenery; (2) for designing costumes; (3) for designing a musical recording studio; (4) for designing musical instruments; and (5) for teaching children to draw music so that they might even grow up to be *artists who specialize in creating music for music publishers.*

This book can also be very helpful to a beginning teacher who has been a music or art major, and who suddenly is faced with the job of becoming a music or art specialist. Finally, this text can be used as a reference or sourcebook by the teacher who wants to illustrate periods in history with appropriate musical examples—and as a reference or sourcebook for units-of-study on the city and its art resources.

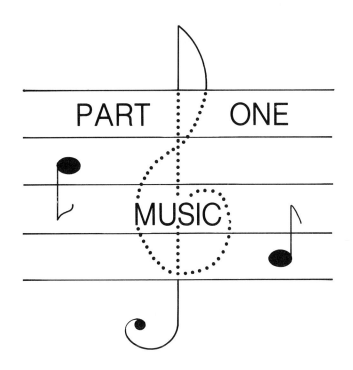

PART ONE

MUSIC

Music Teaching in an Urban Setting

Urban teaching of music involves tremendous excitement as well as severe difficulties. The excitement is derived from the multiplicity of social levels, cultures, and experiences. The difficulties stem from low reading scores, problematic behavior, poor discipline, and cultural barriers (such as not looking at the teacher because of being taught that it is impolite to stare).

Music teaching in the city can be tremendously exciting because youngsters have access to the resources all around them. At the very least, they can tune in stations that broadcast soul, jazz, and Hispanic music—as well as rock, pop, and classical music. At the most, they can be involved in activities which involve actual travel to locations where all these styles are performed or broadcast live.

The urban music teacher may be a "specialist"—but he or she is more likely to be the regular classroom teacher. Urban music teaching may be done in music rooms equipped with the finest musical instruments, or in multipurpose rooms designed for assembly and physical education. One school may have a room filled with electronic pianos. Another may have a small number of broken and battered drums.

In one school, music teaching may have the support of the administration—possibly enough support so that a music specialist is hired or a music specialist position created. In another situation, it is a matter of covering classroom teachers during their preparation periods—the music specialist merely being expected to be a competent disciplinarian so that serious fights or other disturbances do not occur.

In one school, the administration may encourage classroom teachers to teach music (and art)—possibly providing the classroom teacher with songbooks, books of essentials for classroom teachers, and other materials such as this text. In another school, the administration will focus on reading and mathematics, or science.

In one school, music talent may go undiagnosed—even repressed by reactionary teachers and administrators who feel that any sort of banging or drumming on desks is a calculated plot to disrupt a class. In other schools, there is compassion and understanding for the child who is using his energy aesthetically rather than breaking windows, defacing buildings, or mugging old women.

In one school, there can be a chorus and band that equals many performing groups from suburban or rural communities. In other schools, there is no "relevency" of music materials, no excitement in assembly singing, no learning of songflutes, no exploration of chords and harmony through the autoharp or the piano.

The music experiences in the school heavily depend on the resourcefulness, creativity, and enthusiasm of individual teachers—some like yourselves who are being forced or are choosing to take a course that includes the fundamentals and a philosophy of teaching music in an urban setting.

In spite of the possibility that such disparities exist and will continue to exist—especially in the light of continued "white flight" and exodus of both black and white middle class families—there are certain *commonalities* on which the urban elementary music program can be based. They involve the experiences of the city itself: the plethora of record shops; recording displays in department stores; Hispanic and soul radio stations; live jazz spots; concerts in parks or libraries; and location of famous music schools.

For all these aural and visual reasons, enhanced is the meaningfulness of classroom music that includes activities with Latin rhythm instruments—enhanced is the meaningfulness of listening to cassette tapes that include musical examples of soul and jazz as well as classical music—enhanced is the meaningfulness of a classroom teacher trying to become the school music specialist by effectively staging a talent show which includes *merengues, mambos,* or West Indian *regges.*

Geared toward the inner city, this section of the book will face the problems of relevency for urban students when dealing with classroom music or creating specific cassette tapes for use in the listening program of classroom music.

CHAPTER ONE

Classroom Music

Concept: The overall aim and goal of classroom music must be an increase in musicality or "comprehensive-musicianship"—including musical literacy, perceptive listening, performance, and creativity.

Classroom music involves a variety of musical activities. This includes learning music history, analysis, improvisation, playing instruments, and singing. Some musical activities depend upon or are greatly helped by the ability to read music.

READING MUSIC[1]

There are still many societies that do not have a written notation; all of their music is in the oral tradition. We in the Western World are fortunate that we have a system of written music which enables us to play music without first hearing it; yet we also have an added burden of having to learn a language that at times is even more difficult than our spoken tongue. For example, *notes which look the same do not always sound the same.* Sometimes, however, as with homonyms, notes which look different do sound the same.[2] A second source of confusion is that both horizontal and vertical lines are used—horizontal lines for "the staff" itself upon which notes are written; vertical lines for the "stems" of music notes. Finally, there are many different ways of writing eighth and sixteenth notes—the stems sometimes going up on the right side; sometimes down on the left side; sometimes singly written; sometimes connected by twos; and sometimes connected by fours.

Example 1: Different types of eighth notes.

The fact that so many different symbols represent the same concept shows that patience is needed with students who seem confused; it is almost like seeing the alphabet in single, double, quadruple, and upside down. Poor writing of music also adds to confusion, as does poor vision—whether caused by students not wearing glasses or otherwise. (If you wear glasses and wish to get an idea of this problem: write music on the chalkboard; go to the back of the room; take your glasses off; and try to distinguish between notes.)

Although the ability to read music well either depends upon years of study or the use of *many* different beginning music books, *the following basics can be learned in the process of teaching a class.* (Some explanations are written so that they can be read directly to students, if necessary.)

How Notes Look. All notes have "noteheads" which are circles that are either open or filled in. An *open circle alone* is a "whole note." A *circle with a stem* is a "half note." A *filled-in circle with a stem* is a "quarter note." Filled-in circles with stems and either flags or connecting bars are "eighth notes."

Example 2: Noteheads, stems, connecting bars, and flags.

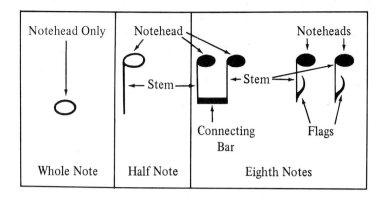

Where Notes Are Placed (lines and spaces). A single "staff" has five lines and four spaces; the "Great Staff" has ten lines. Notes can either be on lines and called "line-notes" or in spaces and called "space-notes." Where notes are placed determines "pitch" (the highness or lowness of sound). It is important to realize that the *notehead determines the exact pitch.* (Where the stems are does not affect the pitch.)

Example 3: Noteheads on lines and in spaces.

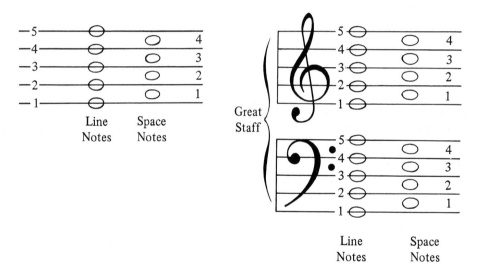

Example 4: Notes with stems on lines and in spaces.

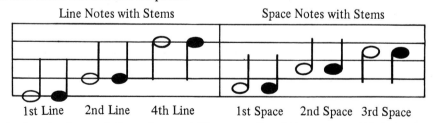

To be sure absolute beginners fully understand "line-notes" and "space-notes" it is best to start with one or two lines.

Example 5: First lesson on line- and space-notes.

A line-note goes both above and below a line. A space-note goes between two lines. Students who sit in back of the room should be asked to come up to the chalkboard, both to read notes, and to draw notes on the board (practicing line-notes *and* space-notes, starting with whole notes on lines, *and* in spaces). It is especially important that urban students, who need (but often are not wearing) their glasses, come up to the board. It is equally important, in urban classrooms, to walk around and check papers; more students than one might think will make errors of perception; and it is part of the inner-city teacher's responsibility (and accountability) to correct those errors of perception. For example, a teacher should make sure space-notes do not go through a line instead of just touching it.

Example 6: Identifying lines and spaces.

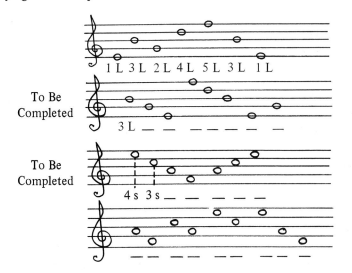

The Musical Alphabet (ABCDEFG). On the lines and in the spaces of "the staff," notes are given ABCDEFG letter-names. The letter-names ABCDEFG come from the names of the lines and spaces themselves as determined by a *clef sign* which tells you what the names of the lines and spaces are. (For example, *the familiar G clef, which evolved from a G placed on the staff, winds around the second line and makes the second line G.* Thus, a note on the second line is G *if the G clef is there*.)

Example 7: The G clef.

The G Clef   The G Clef on the Staff   The G Clef Makes the 2nd Line G

Similarly, the F clef (lower half of "The Great Staff") winds around the fourth line and makes the fourth line F.

Example 8: The F clef.

The F Clef   F Clef on the Staff   The F Clef Makes the 4th Line F

It is important to try to drive home the concept that a note's alphabetical name is determined by a clef. Otherwise, students will be left with the *half-truth that the names of the lines are E G B D F and the spaces are F A C E.*

Example 9: EGBDF—FACE (lines and spaces of the G clef).

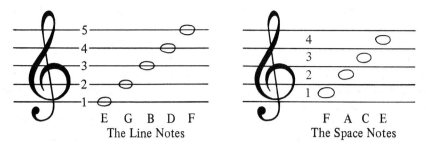

E G B D F
The Line Notes

F A C E
The Space Notes

Although you may wish to remember the lines and spaces of the G clef with *Every Good Boy Does Fine* (EGBDF), and "Face" (FACE), in some ways this method does more harm than good. For example, E is *not* always a line-note (it can be a line-note or a space-note); F is *not* always a space-note (it can be a space-note *or* a line-note). It is much, much preferable to develop the concept that music proceeds from line, to space, to line, to space—using the alphabetical letters A B C D E F G, A B C D E F G, A etc. [3]

Example 10: The musical alphabet on The Great Staff (there is no h, or i through z, in music).

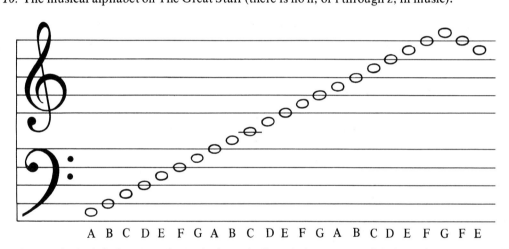

A B C D E F G A B C D E F G A B C D E F G F E

Thus, the musical alphabet goes from A through G and then starts with A again. We may think of the musical alphabet as going *up from A through G;* we may think of the musical alphabet as going *down from G through A.*

EXERCISES FOR THE MUSICAL ALPHABET

The musical alphabet goes up from A _____ ____ .

A B C ____ ____ ____ ____ A.

G F E ____ ____ ____ ____ G.

There is no ____ in music.

We may think of A through G on a staff as going _____ .

We may think of G F E though A on a staff as going _____ .

If adjacent, A is h ____ ____ ____ ____ ____ than G.

If adjacent, G is l ____ ____ ____ ____ than A.

Tempo. Music can be fast or slow; its speed is called "tempo." If music gets faster or slower we say the tempo has changed: the tempo is fast, or the tempo is slow.

As simple as this concept is, historically it was not always this way. Before the eighteenth century the tempo of music was neither very fast nor very slow. Nor did compositions change tempo in the middle of a section; once a section started, it proceeded at that same tempo until the end of the section. The *next* section could then be faster or slower.

Counting Time. As music has tempo or speed, music moves in beats. You can both count the beats and feel the beat. If you count *1 2 3 4, 1 2 3 4* you may feel a march rhythm. If you count 1 2 3, 1 2 3 you feel a waltz rhythm. Often the *tempo* is important as to whether you feel a march or a waltz; if the tempo is too fast or too slow you will not feel like marching even if you count *1 2 3 4, 1 2 3 4*; similarly, if the tempo is much too fast you will not recognize a waltz beat even if you can count *1 2 3, 1 2 3*.

Bar Lines and Measuring Time. The oral tradition of "feeling" the tempo and "the beat" came early in the history of Western Music—long before music was written down. But, while all other cultures retained the oral tradition or a very primitive system of notation, Western cultures evolved a sophisticated system of meters, keys, tempo, and harmony that permitted the creation of such masterpieces as Beethoven's *Fifth Symphony.* Meter is merely a system of grouping beats. In the waltz rhythm that we spoke of—*1 23 1 23* (oom pah pah oom pah)—beats are grouped by threes. When they are grouped by threes the meter can be 3/2, 3/4, or 3/8 (*or any "meter sign" with the top number as three*). The top number of a 3/2, 3/4, or 3/8 meter sign tells you that the musical beat proceeds in threes; the lower number tells you what kind of a note is the basic unit or beat.[4] *If the lower number is four, a quarter note gets a beat. If the lower number is 2, the half note gets a beat. If the lower number is 8 an eighth note gets a beat.*

Measures are ways of grouping beats or measuring time. If we group beats by three, we measure every group of three beats; after every three beats we place a bar line. Example 11 shows an example of 2/4, and 3/4 meters, measures of 2/4 and 3/4 time, and bar lines.

Example 11: 2/4 and 3/4 meters, measures, and bar lines.

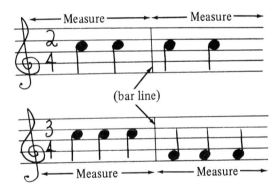

EXERCISES FOR COUNTING TIME

	(Answers)
In 2/4 time (meter is 2/4) there are _____ beats in every measure.	*2*
In 3/4 time (3/4 meter) there are _____ beats in every measure.	*3*
In 4/4 time there are _____ beats in every measure.	*4*
In 4/4 time a _____ note gets one beat.	*quarter*
If the lower note is 4, a quarter note gets _____ beat.	*one*
If the lower note is 2 a _____ _____ gets	*half note*
_____ beat.	*one*

Sharps and Flats, and Key Signatures. A sharp ♯ , when placed before a note, raises the pitch of the note or makes the note higher. *But a sharped note can also be a note in and of itself.* For example, some students think F♯ is F raised a half step without realizing that F ♯ is a note itself.

Example 12:

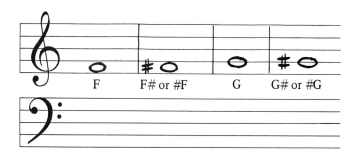

F   F# or #F   G   G# or #G

For example the five different black keys on the piano are sharps: C♯ , D♯ , F♯ , G♯ , A ♯ or (1) A♯ , (2) C♯ , (3) D♯ , (4) F ♯ , (5) G♯ .

Example 13:

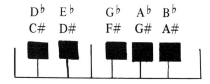

D♭   E♭   G♭   A♭   B♭
C#   D#   F#   G#   A#

They are not merely the same letter names raised although they are that too. F♯ , for example, *is* a black note, and a different key from F natural which is a white key.

EXERCISE   True   False

F♯ is a black key.

F natural is a black key.

G natural is a black key.

G♯ is a black key.

A♯ is a white key.

A flat (♭), when placed before a note, lowers the pitch of the note or makes the note lower. *But a flatted note can also be a note in and of itself.* B♭ is a black key on the piano, as well as the note B lowered 1/2 step. Some students think that B♭ is B lowered, **without** realizing that B♭ is a note itself.

A key signature is a way of grouping the flats and sharps used in a song or composition. The key signature is at the beginning of a song, right after the clef sign. It tells you which flats and sharps to use.

Dynamics. Like tempo, *dynamics* is more recent a concept than many would imagine. Prior to the Baroque Era (seventeenth century) music had melody, harmony, form, texture, and tempo. But just as a section did not get faster and faster or slower, there was no appreciable change in the volume of the music played. In the seventeenth century composers began modifying the dynamics of a piece (loudness or softness). This was done by adding or detracting the number of instruments played at one time. When more instruments played, the music was louder; when fewer were playing the dynamic level was softer or lower. The term for this was "terrace" or "terraced" dynamics.

In music, it is traditional to employ Italian words which indicate various levels of dynamics in music. The Italian word is used which represents the volume at which the music is to be played. On the following page are some common examples.

Italian Word	Abbreviation	English Translation
piano	p	softly
mezzo-piano	mp	moderately soft
pianissimo	pp	very soft
forte	f	loud
mezzo-forte	mf	moderately loud
fortissimo	ff	very loud

LISTENING AND ANALYSIS

Analysis Charts. Musical analysis is not difficult. Even now you can already analyze music in terms of its *tempo, dynamics,* and perhaps *meter.* Thus, you will be able to help a class understand and enjoy music more by feeling that they are able to engage in *musical analysis.* Even before proceeding further, you are now capable of preparing rexographed sheets or planning boardwork with the following format:

Example 14:

Analysis Chart 1

Composition:

Mood or feeling:

Singers or name of group:

Tempo:

Dynamics:

Meter:
 (Educated guess):

Identifying Instruments. A possible early step in musical analysis is the ability to identify instruments that are on recordings you will wish to play for your students, or on cassette tapes that you will learn to prepare in Chapter Two.

Woodwind, Brass Percussion Sections

Woodwind Section and Harp, Also Part of Strings

If you've had thorough courses in music appreciation, either in high school or as an undergraduate, you may be able to identify instruments such as the oboe, bassoon, and French horn. If you've not had the benefit of such a

Oboe

Bassoon

French Horn

course or courses, the task is much more difficult. Yet, you can immediately add a category of "Instruments Used" to the *analysis chart* suggested above (see example 14) by choosing recordings for classroom use that have clearly identifiable instruments—ones which even children can often recognize: drums, guitar, trumpet, piano, bass guitar, harps, saxophone, sometimes the tuba, sometimes the flute, and violin. The Analysis Chart 2 can now be as follows:

Example 15:

Analysis Chart 2

Composition:	Dynamics:
Mood or feeling:	Meter:
Singers or group:	Instruments used: (that are clearly recognizable)
Tempo:	

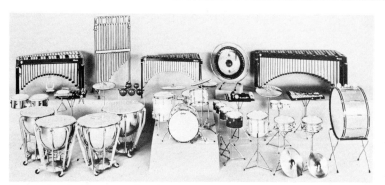

Percussion Instruments Display

Trumpet   Saxophone

Teaching Instrument Recognition. To help students recognize instruments, use *concertos* or *sonatas* that feature solo instruments. If you want students to learn what the clarinet sounds like, rather than picking a short solo from a symphony, play Mozart's *Clarinet Concerto*. Also, to demonstrate the sound of the clarinet, play jazz recordings by Benny Goodman, Artie Shaw, or Woody Herman. Use other sonatas and concertos *rather than excerpts from symphonies*. For example, Mozart wrote a *Horn Concerto in E♭* that will help students learn the sound of the French Horn. The *Oboe Sonata* by Francis Poulenc is excellent.

Two delightful works which feature particular instruments, *Peter and the Wolf* (Prokofiev) and *Carnival of the Animals* (Saint Saens) used to be even more popular than today for use in the classroom. The clarinet, oboe, bassoon, and French horns are particularly recognizable in *Peter and the Wolf*. The piano and cello ("The Swan") receive excellent use in *Carnival of the Animals*.

To teach "instrument recognition" on a regular basis, purchase several record collections specially prepared for children—ones which contain guides for listening and a variety of compositions.[5]

To help students identify instruments you can also retape portions from different works for short quizzes; play parts of string quartets for the sounds of the violin, viola, cello, and double bass; use "contextual-clues" such as the trumpets in the *William Tell Overture* (once heard never forgotten) or the violin solo in *Scheherezade*.

Mozart

Grand Piano

Prokofiev

Rimsky-Korsakov

Clarinet

Cello

Rossini

EXERCISE

1. "The Swan" by Saint-Saens features the

2. In *Peter and the Wolf* birds are represented by the

3. Mozart wrote a   Concerto.

4. Mozart also wrote a  Concerto.

5. Poulenc wrote an  Sonata.

6. Among jazz clarinetists were (*Benny Goodman*), (*Woody Herman*), and (*Artie Shaw*).

7. Probably the most famous jazz trombonist of the swing era was (*Tommy Dorsey*).

8. The tuba can be taught through playing the recording (*Tubby the Tuba*).

TTMMMPPFRHD. There are many *mnemonics* for remembering the factors (or constituent and expressive elements) of music. Some will have to be studied in greater depth (if you do *not* have a background which includes private music-study) for you to be able to help your students analyze music. But here are some of the simpler elements included in a *mnemonic* for remembering what to look for when listening to and analyzing music:

Example 16: Constituent and Expressive Elements of Music.

Texture
Tempo
Meter
Mood
Melody
Performing Media
Phrasing
Form
Rhythm
Harmony
Dynamics

The "textures" of music are generally thought of as *Monophonic* (single line or voice), *homophonic* (one dominant voice), and *polyphonic* (many line or voiced). If the following brief explanation does not enable you to have a mental picture (or hear the sound in your head) by all means consult any good standard text on music appreciation.[6,7] *Monophonic* music is just one single line such as "Gregorian Chant" of the Catholic Church, or many unaccompanied folk songs. Polyphonic music may be thought of as either (a) rounds and canons such as "Row, Row, Row Your Boat" or "Frere Jacques,"; (b) music in which there is considerable counterpoint as in Bach Fugues; or (c) music in which two or more melodies are interwoven such as in the music of Wagner. Homophonic music includes much of the music of Masters such as Haydn, Mozart, Beethoven, Schubert, and Chopin (although these masters *also* wrote considerable contrapuntal or polyphonic music). In homophonic music one voice dominates and the other voices play supporting accompaniment based upon the harmonies of the piece.

ROW, ROW, ROW YOUR BOAT

Moods are often created by a combination of tempo and "mode." "Modes" are scale patterns with differing relationships regarding the size of intervals between notes. The most common "modes" of music are *major* and *minor*. Old-fashioned approaches taught that *major* was "happy" and minor was "sad." This is *not* always true, but if the concept helps you to hear the difference, use it. Minor mode music *if the tempo is slow* does often sound sad; but the minor mode in a fast tempo *can* sound happy. Major mode music usually sounds cheerful *if moderate or fast;* but major mode music in a very slow tempo *can* sound sad also.

With effort or a musical background, you **might** be able to "hear" *the lowered third degree of the scale in the minor mode.* This is the correct way to differentiate music that is *minor* from music that is *major.* One of the *three minor scales* (there is only one major scale) uses a lowered 6th degree and a normal 7th degree—which makes for an Arabian-belly-dancing-type-sound, or snake-charming-sound.

Both the major and minor modes use an eight note scale; both are part of the "diatonic system."[8] The diatonic system is not much older than the practice of "graded dynamics" (extremes in dynamic levels), having achieved widespread usage as recently as the seventeenth century.

Example 17: The major and minor modes (in the Key of C).

Major

Natural. Minor (lowered third, lowered sixth, lowered seventh, same going up and going down).

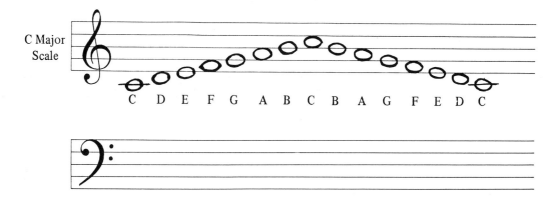

Melodic (different going up and coming down. Up: just lowered third; down: lowered sixth and third).

Harmonic Minor (same going up and coming down, lowered third and sixth, natural seventh).

C Minor
Scale
(Harmonic form)

C D E♭ F G A♭ B C B A♭ G F E♭ D C

Among other "modes" used in music is the pentatonic or five-note scale. If we play only the black keys of the piano we are using the pentatonic scale. Among the familiar songs using a pentatonic scale are "Old MacDonald Had a Farm" and "Auld Lang Syne."

OLD MACDONALD HAD A FARM*

Not dragging

Introduction   U. S.

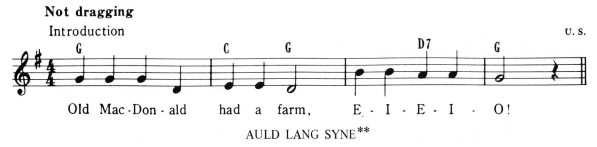

Old Mac-Don-ald   had   a   farm,   E - I - E - I - O!

AULD LANG SYNE**

ROBERT BURNS   SCOTLAND

With nostalgia

1. Should auld   ac-quaint-ance   be   for-got, And   nev-er brought to

mind? Should auld   ac-quaint-ance   be   for-got, And   days of auld lang syne?

Identifying Period or Style. Identifying style is often difficult, even for a trained musician, and may be beyond the scope of most elementary school classrooms. For gifted students, however, there are some ways to go about attempting to include style or period in an "Analysis Chart." First, there are what may loosely be called "educated guesses." For example, if we are told that Bach, Vivaldi, and Handel were composers of the Baroque Period, any time we hear a piece we already know by these composers it can be labeled "Baroque Music." Then, if we hear a work that seems also to be by these composers or seems to have the same style, we can "guess" that the music is also from the Baroque Era. Regarding contemporary music, we can learn that if an orchestra is very, very large with many, many pieces of percussion, we can be fairly sure the work is from the twentieth century or by a twentieth century composer. The style of the Viennese Classical Period (1750-1820 roughly) is difficult to analyze at times. Yet if we hear enough music by Haydn, Mozart, and early Beethoven *we can associate the sound of the music with the period.* (The music is diatonic, and the full orchestra is used; but it is not a large orchestra and there are no tubas and not many trombones.)

*To "play only on the black keys," change all notes to flats.
**To "play only on the black keys," change all notes to sharps.

Bach

Vivaldi

Handel

Haydn

Mozart

Beethoven

Identifying Composers. Musical analysis in depth cannot be done easily in an elementary school classroom; it is difficult even for many undergraduates. But fifth and sixth graders *can* identify composers through "differentiation"—and this later will serve as a basis for identification of composers based upon aspects of their style. Moreover, in the process of differentiating between composers, students will be *nonverbally* "thinking through" musical aspects of the compositions to be compared. (In this respect, frequent repetition is essential.)

Example 18:

Analysis Chart 3

Composition	Dynamics
Mood or feeling	Composer
Melody or harmony	Reasons for choosing composer:
Texture	1.
	2.
Tempo	3.
Medium	

Identifying Forms. Fifth and sixth graders can analyze some musical forms, without having to probe deeply into the *structure* of a composition. For example, start with simple songs in which there is an introduction, before the main part of the record begins. Identify this as "Intro——song" and call it *A B form.* Proceed next to songs where there is some kind of an ending, as well as the introduction. Identify this as "Intro——Song——Ending" and call it *A B C form.* With practice, youngsters may develop ability to identify longer forms, such as A B, A C, A B A (which is called a *rondo*).

Identifying Melodic Invention. Analysis of many melodic patterns is beyond the scope of the elementary school classroom. However, elementary school children *can* identify the following characteristics of melodies. Whether melodies used: (1) move by small steps or large skips; (2) are long and smooth or short and jagged; (3) move in very fast notes, even if the tempo is slow; (4) move in very long notes, even if the tempo is very fast.

Example 19: Slow tempo but fast notes.

Example 20: Fast tempo but long notes.

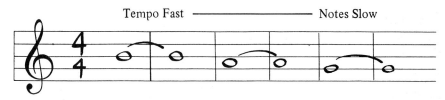

Example 21: Stepwise motion.

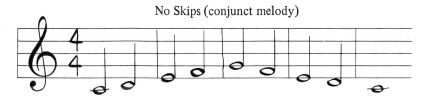

Example 22: Large skips.

SINGING

Singing has always been a part of classroom music; but, in recent years there has been added emphasis on relevancy and use of material that students really want to sing. The idea is not to try to change "taste" *head-on,* as was done in the past; rather, gradually to bridge the gap between the past and the present, and to seize upon strong interest in current music. (See also Chapter Two p. 41.)

Use of Pop Songs. There are many popular recordings to which students will want to dance, and which students will want to sing. The teacher is wise to show acceptance and to capitalize on this intrinsic motivation. Using well-liked songs, several activities can follow—and there will be an accompanying student desire to: (1) observe written notation for particular songs, as they're played in the background; (2) sing favorite songs,

without the songs being played in the background; (3) analyze the songs or reproduce some of their rhythms on the drums; and (4) make one's **own** class recording on a cassette tape. (See Chapter Two.)

EXERCISE

Make a transparency of the music for a popular song.

Write a plan for teaching children to sing a popular song without the recording being played in the background.

Make an "Analysis Chart" for a popular song.

Play a popular song on the guitar or piano.

Make a cassette recording of a song you feel children would like to sing. (See Chapter Two pp. 41-43.)

Church, Religious, or Holiday Songs. Because of familiarity, perhaps, another category of songs which one can get children to sing with little effort is "religious or holiday songs." (We learn through "repetition" and once learned we feel most comfortable with that which we know.) Many children who resist learning new songs (folk and/or classical) often join in with "Jingle Bells," "Go Tell It on the Mountain," or "Every Time I Feel the Spirit."

JINGLE BELLS

J. PIERPONT

Jin - gle bells,   jin - gle bells,   jin - gle   all   the   way.

GO TELL IT ON THE MOUNTAIN

SPIRITUAL

1. When   I   was   a   seek - er,   I   sought both night and   day ;   I

EVERY TIME I FEEL THE SPIRIT

SPIRITUAL

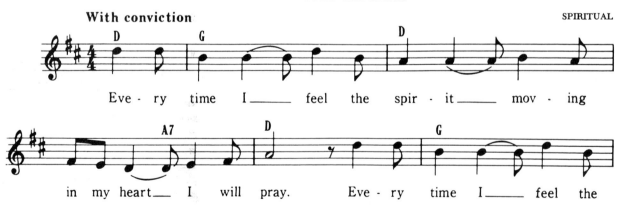

Eve - ry   time   I ____ feel   the   spir - it ____ mov - ing

in   my   heart __   I   will   pray.   Eve - ry   time   I ____ feel   the

EXERCISE

List other religious or holiday songs which you have found students are anxious or at least willing to sing.

1.   4.

2.   5.

3.   6.

7.   9.

8.   10.

Camp, or Game Songs. Another category of songs children often sing without the teacher having to work hard at "motivation" is *camp songs*. This is another area to explore, especially if you feel you won't be able to get the children to sing (especially boys in the fifth and sixth grades). Among such songs are "I've Been Working On the Railroad," and "John Jacob Jingleheimer Schmidt." (In the schoolyards of big cities, or outside the school, children sing a type of inner-city folk song to which they often jump rope or do a dance. Included in such songs are "Miss Lucy Had a Steamboat," "Head 'n' Shoulders," and "Hambone.")

I'VE BEEN WORKING ON THE RAILROAD

Di - nah won't you blow, Di - nah won't you blow your horn? Some-one's in the kitch-en with Di - nah, Some-one's in the kitch-en I know, Some-one's in the kitch-en with Di - nah, Strum-ming on the old ban jo. Fee fie fid-dle-ee - i - o, Fee fie fid-dle-ee - i - o, Fee fie fid-dle-ee - i - o, Strum-ming on the old ban - jo.

JOHN JACOB JINGLEHEIMER SCHMIDT

CAMP SONG

John Ja - cob Jing - le-heim - er Schmidt, That's my name

too!   When - ev - er I go out,   the peop - ple al - ways shout,

John   Ja - cob Jing-le- heim - er Schmidt Da da da da da da da   da.

EXERCISE

List at least five songs children sing at camp.

1.   4.

2.   5.

3.

List at least four songs children sing out of school while playing games.

1.   3.

2.   4.

Make a cassette tape, *Side One* to contain children singing "camp songs," *Side Two* children singing "game songs."

Folk Songs. There are many, many excellent filmstrips on the Revolutionary or Civil Wars which include folk songs. Don't plan to worry if children won't sing along at first; it will be only with repetition that the songs will become familiar enough for them to feel comfortable with the words; *then* they will start singing.

THE BLUE TAIL FLY

DAN EMMETT   U. S.

1. When I was young I   used to wait on mas-ter and give him his plate, And

CAMPTOWN RACES

STEPHEN C. FOSTER   STEPHEN C. FOSTER

1. The Camp-town la - dies sing this song,   do - da,   do - da! The

BUFFALO GALS

COOL WHITE

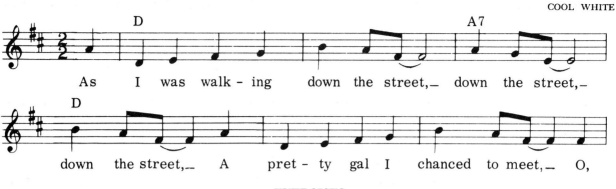

As   I   was   walk - ing   down   the   street,__   down   the   street,__

down   the   street,__   A   pret - ty   gal   I   chanced   to   meet,__   O,

EXERCISES

Ask a school librarian if she has filmstrips with folk songs on them.

List three filmstrips which include folk songs.

Write to a City Music Bureau or State Education Department for a recommendation of filmstrips which include folk songs.

Explore issues of Music Education Journals for advertisements of filmstrips which use folk songs.

Easy-to-Sing Classics. A desirable and recommended objective is the singing of some classical literature. *But,* you may say, children will wrinkle their noses and say *Ugh.* Perhaps you will have to seek classics with a small enough range or simple enough rhythm. Among such literature is the "Ode to Joy" from Beethoven's Ninth Symphony or the songs from Humperdink's *Hansel and Gretel* (an opera for children).

EXERCISE

Name a music series which includes the "Ode to Joy" or a song from *Hansel and Gretel.* (Is there an accompanying record to demonstrate the song?)

_____ City: _____

Publisher: _____ .

Vocalizes. A "vocalize" is a set of neutral syllables used for voice training, e.g., loo loo loo loo loo loo loo loo loo.

Example 23:

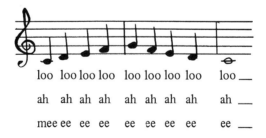

loo loo loo loo   loo loo loo loo   loo __

ah ah ah ah   ah ah ah ah   ah __

mee ee ee ee   ee ee ee ee   ee __

Many times, students will sing a "vocalize" for two reasons: one, they find it funny, and this relaxes them enough to sing and giggle; two, there are no difficult words for them to remember and the absence of feeling threatened enables them to sing along. Make it *fun* and a game.

EXERCISE

Obtain permission to use a *vocalize* with a fifth grade class, and describe what happens (be brief, but include

facial expressions and comments which students call out). _____

_____

Kodaly Hand Signs. Zoltan Kodaly was a Hungarian educator and composer who perfected a system of hand signs for use in teaching music. They are used in conjunction with Italian (originally Latin) syllable names for the scale.

Do	Re	Mi	Fa	Sol	La	Ti	Do
C	D	E	F	G	A	B	C

Future teachers who plan to emphasize or include singing should consult references giving complete descriptions of this excellent method.

RHYTHMIC ACTIVITIES

Much of the material on "Reading Music" dealt with rhythm (especially sections on "tempo," "meter," "counting time," and "measures and barlines"). But the *Rhythmic Activities* suggested here involve a more active participation in the *kinesthetics* of rhythm: how it *feels*. Basically then, rhythmic activities can be subdivided into two groups: emphasis on *activities,* or emphasis on concepts about *rhythm*. Rhythmic *activities* can involve anything from musical chairs, to social or square dancing, to using batons and "conducting" recorded music.

Musical Chairs. A game in which every time the music stops you sit down on chairs that are short by one. The child who fails to find a chair is out.

Social Dancing. Use of the latest recordings. Hopefully, boys will dance with girls.

Square Dancing. A very worthwhile rhythmic activity. Special skills are required from "how to" books on square dancing; sometimes recordings can be used which explain the steps; some films are available also.

BOW BELINDA

LOOBY LOO

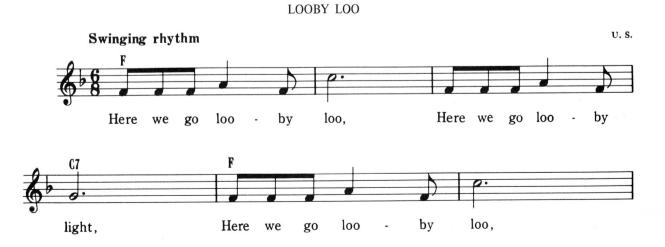

PAWPAW PATCH

FROG WENT A-COURTING

Folk or Ethnic Dancing. Dances such as the *Italian Tarentella, Irish Jig, Polish Polka, Israeli Horra,* Greek Dances, African Dances, etc. Special skills are required, but, again, some recordings teach the steps, as do some films.

Conducting 2/4, 3/4, or 4/4 Patterns. A "feel" for certain basic conducting patterns can be taught easily. The 2/4 pattern is little more than "down-up" repeated over and over again.

Example 24: 2/4 Conducting pattern.

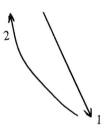

The 3/4 conducting pattern is: "Down—To The Right—Then Up."

Example 25: 3/4 Conducting pattern.

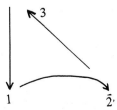

The 4/4 conducting pattern is: "Down—To The Left—To The Right—Then Up."

Example 26: 4/4 Conducting pattern.

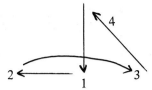

The Orff System. To be explained briefly on page 28. The Orff system is wonderful for developing rhythmic awareness and sensitivity.

The Dalcroze System. The Dalcroze system of "Eurythmics" is another exceedingly important contribution to music education. It should be studied if you feel strongly about emphasizing the rhythmic aspects of music to children.

Dynamics as Rhythm. "Dynamics," as you may recall, refers to the *louds and softs of music,* and is not really part of the concept of rhythm. In actual practice, however, the process of trying to indicate loud or soft through one's conducting gestures has a rhythmic "feel" and is an aspect of the rhythm of conducting.

Upbeats. Another aspect of "the rhythm of conducting" is the principle of an *upbeat.* Since many songs start on an upbeat, it is worthwhile to practice the gesture (or motion) of going up before each of the conducting patterns for 2/4, 3/4, and 4/4. It is particularly important to practice the upbeat before the 3/4 pattern, because the *Star Spangled Banner* begins this way.

Negating Beats. Another important aspect of rhythm is the "rest" (the absence of sound) while a rhythmic impulse continues. The "rest" not only plays an important role in reading music, but also in conducting music. Conducting rests involves "negating" or *minimizing beats, so that instrumentalists or vocalists actually see where they are to stop.*

Before doing the exercises below, let's consider an important second way of conducting the meters 2/4, 3/4, and 4/4. In this method, only the last beat is up; *all* other beats are down: e.g., down-up; down-down-up; and down-down-down-up. Moreover, even the last beat starts by going down; *but,* there is a rubbery rebound which makes the beat rapidly go up. Thus, "down-up" becomes "Push, Push-bounce." "Down-down-up" becomes "Push, Push Push-bounce."

In the following exercises, eliminate (*negate or minimize*) a beat every time you see a rest by making only a very small gesture for the rest.

EXERCISE

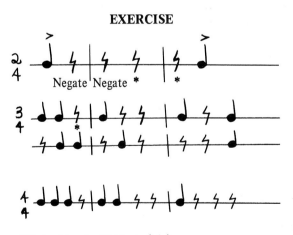

*Note: Negate All Rests (𝄾)

CLASSROOM INSTRUMENTS

Traditionally, classroom instruments have been those that were not difficult to blow into, fairly portable, not expensive, generally easy to play, and which clearly illustrated basic music concepts. Among the more popular classroom instruments, therefore, have been recorders, autoharps, Swiss melode bells, and resonator bells. In recent years, Hispanic and African instruments such as the Kalimba have entered the repertory of classroom instruments.

Orff Instruments. It is beyond the scope of this book to explain the "Orff-Schulwerk System" (originated by Karl Orff, the German musicologist and composer of *Carmina Burana*). It is urged, however, that classroom teachers take courses or attend workshops devoted to this method. References can be cited; but it is best to benefit directly by being physically present when an expert clinician demonstrates the approach; it is only a live demonstration that truly communicates a feeling for what it is all about.

Part of the Orff system involves special instruments, although a working knowledge of the approach will enable you to incorporate the system in your teaching, even if you *don't* have the special instruments. Some of the instruments are expensive; but the entire array can be purchased for the cost of a piano—and if they are purchased more students will be involved in performance (even singing) than if the money was used for purchase of a piano.

Like the Kodaly system, the Orff approach starts with folk material and songs which are in the pentatonic scale.

Wall Bells

Swiss Melode Bells. There are several advantages of using melode bells: (1) they are small and portable; (2) the tones can be arranged for playing melodies without having to skip from one tone to another; (3) they are color coded for building concepts of different pitches; and (4) they are so inexpensive that everyone in a class can have one bell or even a set. No special ability is needed for using them; even a teacher with *no* musical background can help students develop musicality and learn to read music through their use. A booklet is almost always included with each set that has several songs with musical notes in different colors (to parallel the bells) and also using numbers and letter names.

The Melode Bells. (The tone is created by shaking the bell, holding it from the top.)

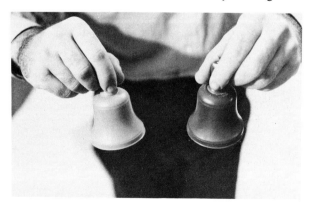

The actual pitches of the swiss-type melode bells are F G A B♭ C D E F. This is the "F Major Scale"—the B♭ makes for the half step between the third and fourth tones—which you may remember is a diatonic scale.

Example 27: The F major scale.

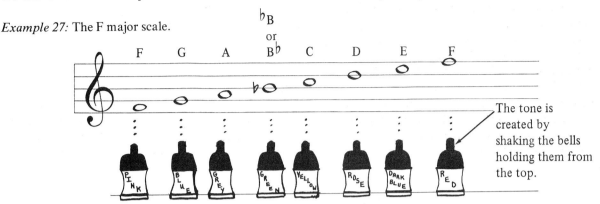

The tone is created by shaking the bells holding them from the top.

Another way of using the swiss-type melode bells is for teaching *harmony.* Two or more bells can be played simultaneously either by different students or the same student.[9]

Tone-Educator or Resonator Bells. Everything said about the swiss-type melode bells is true of the Tone-Educator or Resonator Bells—with the exception that they are not quite so inexpensive. Each bell can be removed from the case individually. In addition, like the piano, they are *chromatic*—which means that they have all the sharps and flats as well as the natural notes or white keys.

Figure 1. Resonator bells.

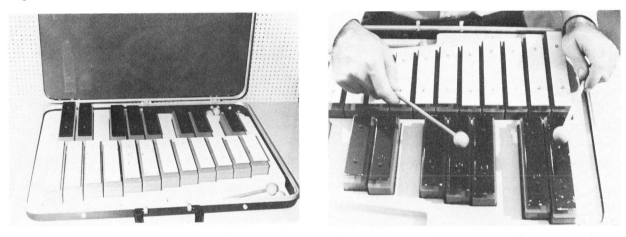

The Chromatic Pitch Pipe. From the Greek word *Chroma,* meaning color, chromatic notes are the sharps and flats which "color the scale." Chromatic also means moving in 1/2 steps such as going up as C C♯ D D♯ E F F♯ G G♯ A A♯ B C or coming down C B B♭ A A♭ G G♭ F E E♭ D D♭ C.

Figure 2. Chromatic pitch pipe.

McCOOK COMMUNITY COLLEGE
Learning Resource Center

19340

E to F and B to C are already half steps—and no sharps or flats are needed. In all the other cases sharps and flats *are* needed; C to C♯ is a half step for example; B to B♭ is a half step.

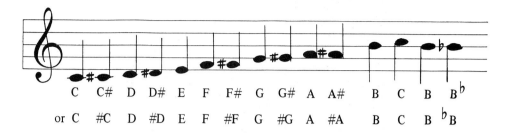

C	C#	D	D#	E	F	F#	G	G#	A	A#	B	C	B	B♭
or C	#C	D	#D	E	F	#F	G	#G	A	#A	B	C	B	♭B

The chromatic pitch pipe will enable you to get any chromatic note; it will enable you to play 1/2 steps going up *or* down the scale; it will enable to learn and teach the chromatic or 1/2 step scale.

Recorders, Flutophones, or Songflutes. Traditionally, one of the favored ways to prepare students for orchestral instruments (particularly woodwinds) is through use of recorders, songflutes, or flutophones. Even second or third graders can play them, because of their small size and because no reeds are needed. Moreover, flutophones and songflutes are rather inexpensive; thus, with low cost, each child in an entire class can have one.

Figure 3. Flutophone.

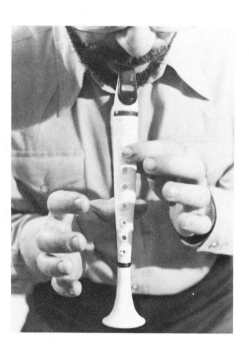

Songflutes and flutophones usually come with a fingering chart and booklet of several songs. Comprehensive guides on essentials for classroom teachers (such as that by Winslow and Dallin[10]) explain fingerings in detail, and should be studied if you seriously intend to use these easy-to-play instruments in your teaching—as you should. The time spent learning them is well worth the effort.

Recorders, songflutes, and flutophones should be used to teach the habit of following a conductor, as well as to teach reading music. They can also be used with classroom singing to help students learn harmony parts, or learn new songs.

The Guitar. The guitar is an excellent classroom instrument, because of its popularity—and because it can be amplified (thus increasing its motivational value). As with our brief discussion of song flutes and flutophones, we will not attempt to teach chord positions in the limited space available. Increasingly, there are many good books which teach the guitar quite simply.

In addition to value as an accompaniment to singing, and classroom use in general, a guitar is an excellent instrument with which to teach concepts of half and whole steps, and harmony.

Figure 4. The guitar.

Latin Percussion Instruments. It cannot be assumed that urban students can automatically play instruments such as the bongos, conga, timbales, cowbell, maracas, or claves. Many maracas have been broken by students who banged them together.

(Although it would be best for classwork to include demonstration of the instruments listed below, the description that follows may help future and present classroom teachers avoid drawing a "total blank" when confronted with their use.)

(1) *Claves.* The easiest Latin percussion instrument to play is the set of sticks called the *claves.* One stick is held in the left hand, resting gently on a cupped palm; the other stick is used to strike the first stick. Despite the ostensible ease, you must have your left hand cupped properly under the stick; otherwise, the proper sound will not occur; and the proper sound is a vibrant, high-pitched click rather than a dull thud.

Figure 5. Claves.

The most typical rhythm of the *claves* is sometimes nicknamed the "shave-and-a-haircut" rhythm.

Example 28:

Shave and a   Hair-Cut

(2) *The Cowbell.* The cowbell can be held by the left hand and struck with a stick held by the right hand.

Figure 6. Cowbell.

One typical cowbell rhythm is "quarter eighth-eighth, quarter eighth-eighth" with the quarter note struck hard with the full stick, then the eighth notes tapped lightly with the tip of the stick.

Example 29: Cha cha rhythm.

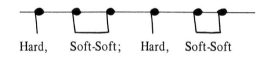

Hard,   Soft-Soft;   Hard,   Soft-Soft

Another typical rhythm for the cowbell is one used for *mambos.*

Example 30: Mambo rhythm.

(3) *The Conga.* The *conga* is large and rather expensive ($80-$200) if you want one with a quality sound. The skin must be tight, but not too tight or it will snap—and the skin should be loosened at the end of the day.

Figure 7. The conga.

To play a typical *conga* rhythm of: "rest; quarter; rest; eighth-eighth"—the center of the conga is struck strongly with the entire palm; then the edge of the skin is tapped sharply with the tips of the fingers (see example 31).

Example 31: Conga rhythm.

Palm   Tip Tip   Palm   Tip Tip

(4) *Bongos.* Bongos can be purchased in sets fairly inexpensively. The bongo rhythms used are sometimes the same as the *conga;* at other times straight eighth or sixteenth notes are employed (see example 32).

Example 32: Bongo rhythm.

The *bongos* are held between the knees if loose and not on a stand. They are often played with one or two fingers of each hand.

Figure 8. Bongos.

(5) *Timbales.* The timbales are two drums held together on a stand. Often they are used in conjunction with a full drum set (bass, snare, hi-hat, ride cymbal, and tom toms). They are usually played with sticks, one stick striking the outside or rim, the other striking the two skins or drumheads alternately:

Example 33: Timbales rhythm.

Rim
Head

For *merengues,* beats such as the following are used:

Example 34: Merengue rhythm.

Figure 9. Timbales.

(6) *Guiro.* Pronounced "Gweedo" the *Guiro* is used very effectively for *cha chas* with the following rhythm:

Example 35: Guiro rhythm.

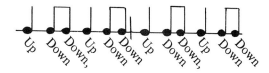

In this *guiro* rhythm, the quarter note is played by moving a stick over the ridges of the *guiro* slowly; then, for the eighth notes, the stick is moved swiftly in the opposite direction. Professionals actually change direction for every note, but it is much harder that way (see example 36).

Example 36: Guiro rhythm.

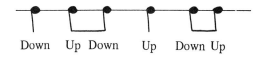

Figure 10. The guiro.

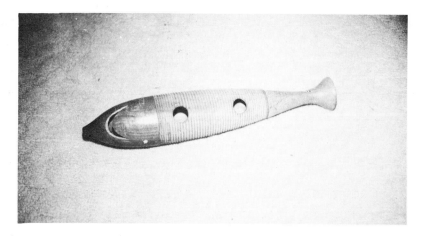

The Autoharp. The autoharp is a traditional classroom instrument that is marvelous for teaching an introduction to harmony and chords. When using the instrument, students only have to press down buttons and "strum" (provided that the instrument has been tuned) in order to play chords and chord progressions. Chords and progressions such as F, D minor, C^7, are played automatically. Once shown how to play it, talented students can act as accompanists for classroom singing—even for a chorus. And this is especially important if there is no piano.

Figure 11. Autoharp.

CREATIVITY

Creativity can include expressive interpretation of music, or synthesis—but creativity usually is thought of as original creation or a unique way of doing something. Creativity should be taught as including slight variations as well as uniqueness.

Poetry and Music. Students can set poetry to music in a variety of ways, including improvisation as well as with written versions. Improvisations can include making up melodies to well-known or original poems, or making up new lyrics to well-known melodies. Using notation for creative process with young children is much more difficult; but it can be done by choosing poems which call only for half and quarter notes (such as "Twinkle Twinkle Little Star," or Schiller's "Ode to Joy" which was used in Beethoven's *Ninth Symphony*.)

TWINKLE, TWINKLE, LITTLE STAR*

Example 37:

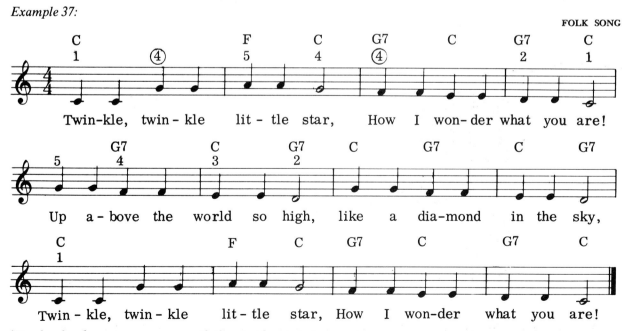

*May be played or sung as a canon—with the second part starting
one measure after the first part.

Example 38:

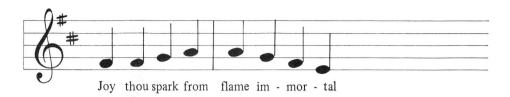

Joy thou spark from flame im - mor - tal

Painting to Music (or improvising music according to paintings). Just as Moussorgsky composed music to specific paintings in *Pictures at an Exhibition,* students can create musical improvisations based upon art works. First, students can paint or draw to different kinds of music, with the goal of reflecting different moods in their art work. (Filmstrips of historical periods can be shown, as an overall introduction to the contrasting of styles—e.g., the darkness of Rembrandt with the lightness of Manet or Degas.) Second, students can improvise sounds which they feel reflect paintings, through singing and/or playing. One can play Moussorgsky's *Pictures at an Exhibition* and point out that the musical sections are based upon a collection of paintings that were being exhibited.

Rhythmic Creativity. Although rhythm is covered in several other sections, rhythmic creativity can be an entity unto itself, in the sense of free body movements in response to a variety of music played. To emphasize rhythm rather than *just* free dance interpretation, however, specific meters such as 2/4, 3/4, or 4/4 can be alternated.

Electronic Creation. To get a basic concept of creating electronic music, simple electronic sounds can be recorded on reel-to-reel or cassette tape. (Reel-to-reel is preferable because "splicing" can be done at a later date, and splicing is an important aspect of the creative process used by professionals in their compositions.) Among the sounds that can be recorded, even **without** using sophisticated equipment, are: (a) the sounds of a push-button telephone; (b) the sound of a telephone left off the receiver too long; (c) "feedback" heard when the tape recorder microphone moves too near the tape recorder speaker; (d) the type of "white noise" obtained by blowing into the microphone; (e) the "distorted sounds" resulting from recording anything much too loud; (f) the sounds of an old recording played on the wrong speed—such as a 33 1/3 record played at 78; (g) the sound of a reel-to-reel tape recording being run backwards; (h) the sound of an old (*unneeded*) recording being artificially forced to play backwards; (i) the sound of running water recorded at a low speed; (j) the sounds of radio static, or the rapid moving of the radio dial from station to station.

MUSIC HISTORY

Musical literacy should include a general idea that: (a) there were distinct "periods" in the history of Western art music; and (b) other cultures have given birth to musical systems and styles totally different from that of Western Europe. Even if students are no more than exposed to the names of musical periods, knowledge will have been communicated about our musical heritage. And even if you can do no more than play a recording of the music of India, China, Japan, or West Africa, you will have helped expose students to the *World's world of sound.*

Western Music, a Broad Overview. Among simple rote tasks for students is the copying of a list of the major periods in Western art music. (As an initial exposure, this ostensible busy work is important and should not be frowned upon.)

Estimated Dates	Period Name (most often used)	Pronunciation
c. 400-c. 1400	Medieval*	Med-ee-evil
1400-1600	Renaissance	Ren-a-sahnce
1400-1750	Baroque	B-roke
1750-1820	Viennese Classical	Vee-a-neese Classical
1820-1900	Romantic	
1860s-1940s	Impressionism	

*Dates vary greatly.

1880s-present	Expressionism	
	Dada	Dah-Dah
	Gebrauchsmusik	Ge-brow-sh-mus-eek
1920s-present	Bruitissimo or	Broo-tee-simo
	Machine Music	
1920s-present	Neo-Classicism	
1920s-present	Neo-Romanticism	
1920s-present	Neo-Nationalism	
1923-present	12-note or	
	Dodecaphonic	
1930s-present	Serial Music	
1940s-present	Chance Music	
1950s-present	Aleatoric Music	
1950s-present	Electronic Music	
	and	
	Musique Concrète	Mu-seek Concrete

Ethno-Musicology Introduction. For a simple introduction to the concept that "there are many diverse styles of music in the world," short excerpts from musics of major cultures can be used: There are many recordings available; and these excerpts can be played while learning about the history of different countries; or the excerpts can be compared with each other for their "sounds." Among the major non-Western cultures whose music is available are India, Iran, Japan, China, and Indonesia. Recordings of African music are often subdivided into North, Central, East, and South because the continent is so vast; and recordings are increasingly available. European music which uses "different" sounding scale and rhythm patterns (and which is often included in recordings which emphasize comparison of diverse styles) includes music of Greece and Turkey—and Irish and Scottish bagpipe music. (When teaching in urban areas—in addition to Black and Hispanic musics—Italian, Irish, Polish, Greek, Jewish, Arabic, Chinese, and Japanese music should also be included.)

Periods in Western Art Music. Facts about classical music become more meaningful during, or related to, listening to actual music itself. (See Chapter 2, pp. 51-52.) However, we sometimes forget to present a historical overview to children when playing and analyzing music. "Musical literacy" should include a general idea of *when* the music we hear was created. The following paragraphs contain suggestions for helping children chronologically "place" Medieval through Romantic music.

To place Medieval music chronologically, we might show pictures of castles and knights in shining armor. We can relate the sounds of the music to the mental images of courtyard bands and jesters. For an even more vivid image we can allude to the Crusades. (When the students become older, the mental stepping stones can be discarded and they will be able to understand specific analytical aspects of the music itself—melodic and rhythmic modes, tempus perfectum etc.).

To help children place Renaissance music historically (1400-1600) we might draw a mental picture of the end of the Crusades, the circumnavigation of the globe, the influence of Marco Polo, or the sunny atmosphere of the great Italian churches. We might show paintings and sketches by Leonardo DaVinci (Last Supper) or Michelangelo. If students have learned about Martin Luther and the Reformation, such facts can be included.

To place Baroque music, historically (1600-1750), we might point out that this was a time when Plymouth Rock (1620) and Jamestown (1607) were settled—and relate the Baroque Era to the Counter-Reformation. We might mention a convenient date of 1600 for a generally agreed-upon beginning for the Baroque Era. (Although too many names [such as Palestrina for the Renaissance] out of context will easily be forgotten—one might mention Bach and Handel as among the giants of Baroque music.)

Bach

Handel

With "Viennese Classicism" or the Classical Era (1750-1820), we might begin to refer to strictly musical events—the death of Johann Sebastian Bach (1750), the influence of Bach's sons, the musical genius of Haydn, Mozart, and Beethoven. Or, as with other periods, we can also describe nonmusical events and characterize the period as one in which the American and French Revolutions took place, as did the War of 1812. We might begin to tie in musical analysis by mentioning that this was the period in music in which real changes in tempo and dynamics took place. (See page 9 and page 10.)

Haydn

Mozart

Beethoven

When you get to "Romanticism" of the nineteenth century, be sure to emphasize the specific use of the term to characterize a century. Many children will find the term humorous and overemphasize the image of lovesick poets such as Keats, Byron, and Shelly. However, musical Romanticists such as Schubert, Tchaikovsky, Wagner, and Chopin can be woven into this conceptual fabric. Historical facts such as the Civil War can help children place the era chronologically. Musical facts should be included such as the expansion of the orchestra and the greater use of chromaticism.

Schubert

Tchaikovsky

Wagner

Chopin

Notes for Chapter One

1. One of the things college students often regret most, about school music, is not having learned to read properly.
2. *Clefs* and *time-signatures* change notes so that their pitch (highness or lowness) and duration (how long a note is held) are modified.
3. Note that *if adjacent A is always higher than G and G is always lower than A.*
4. At this point unlearn the myth that a whole note always gets four beats, if you were taught this way—even though you may have to teach children this way in the beginning to avoid confusion.
5. Recommended: *Adventures in Music* by Gladys Tipton (R.C.A. Victor); The Bowmar record guides for children (Bowmar Publishers).
6. Joseph Machlis. *The Enjoyment of Music* (New York: W.W. Norton & Company, 1970).
7. Homer Ulrich. *Music a Design for Listening* (New York: Harcourt Brace & World, Inc., 1957).
8. Although major and minor are also "modes," we call music "modal" which does not use the diatonic system nor modern chromaticism (an abundance of sharps and flats). Modal music is a return to the old church modes in which few sharps and flats are used only for voice-leading.
9. For additional explanation and pictures see Robert W. Winslow and Leon Dallin, *Music Skills for Classroom Teachers* (Dubuque: Wm. C. Brown Company Publishers, 1971, 3rd ed.), p. 133.
10. *Op. cit., Music Skills for Classroom Teachers.*

CHAPTER TWO

Creating Cassette Tapes
Dealing with a Variety of Musical Styles

Concept: Short excerpts of diverse styles on prerecorded tapes can be used for exciting presentation and comparison of musical variety.

The central theme of this chapter is that a cassette-tape listening program (created and structured by classroom teachers and paraprofessionals) should include popular music; it should then proceed from popular music through jazz, to light classics, finally ending with classical music. Initial exposures to music should use the approach of "identification and comparison"—rather than differentiation between bad or good. It is suggested that the teacher and/or paraprofessional tape a wide variety of *short* excerpts from recordings and/or the radio—introducing each excerpt simply by identifying the style, or by somewhat describing the style in more depth to the children.

Basically, therefore, this chapter includes short descriptions of diverse musical styles and subcategories. The listings and brief descriptions are meant more to illustrate how many different styles there are from which to choose, rather than to thoroughly analyze all of them. In some cases, material is presented that can be incorporated in the verbal introduction to the tape recording (cassette); in some cases a category is mentioned briefly—and the interested teacher will have to do further investigation (in order to understand enough to be able to make an intelligent introduction of a musical excerpt).

Except where absolutely necessary, an attempt has been made *not* to specify singers or groups which exemplify the style in question; the reason is that many performers quickly go out of fashion. However, some musical styles *cannot* be described properly without mentioning the vocalists who best represent them.

As for the process of making the cassette tapes, getting the necessary recordings and making the cassettes may seem like a lot of work—but once having created the tapes, the problem of teaching music appreciation will be *much* easier. The tapes you make now will be your *prerecorded lessons* for a class. On the tape, try to present a little about the musical excerpt the students are about to hear—what style it represents and why it was selected. The overall aim is to present the variety of music; the overall approach is to take the guesswork out of bringing a record to class, and "fishing for the excerpt to be played."

The first side (Side 1) should be examples of popular music. Choose at least five or six three-minute excerpts that are quite different from each other. Depending upon how much talking you do on the tape, the side should last 20 or 30 minutes, perhaps as much as an hour if you choose more subcategories and have more than one example of each. Side 2 will be excerpts from, and your introduction to, different kinds of jazz. Side 3 will be excerpts from, and your introduction to, different styles of folk music; Side 4 will be Light Classical; Side 5, Classical.

The following are the categories from which you may choose, including material you can read to the children:

POPULAR MUSIC (*Side 1*)

Almost everyone knows basically what is meant by popular music. Popular music, as illustrated by *Side One,* contains a variety of popular styles, all of which are somewhat of a commercial success.

Pop. The first category, "pop," is the *most* popular of popular music, in the sense of sales or appealing to largest numbers. Often, other styles of popular music become "pop" if a recording sells enough copies. Pop, therefore, is anything that is "middle-of-the-road" or on the top 40 list of best selling recordings.

Rock. Rock is a large category of popular music. It began as an offshoot of "Rock 'n' Roll" but soon developed into a complete style of its own—with its own substyles of hard-rock, soft-rock, acid-rock, rockabilly, folk-rock, jazz-rock, and psychedelic rock. Although often associated with loud amplified guitars, organs, and synthesizers—rock (as a general style) contains considerable variety within itself. Among early groups and artists associated with rock were The Beatles, Rascals, Rolling Stones, Cream, The Who, Janis Joplin, and Jimi Hendrix. The subject matter of rock includes drugs and protest, as well as traditional love themes.

Soul. Most often, but not always, soul has been associated with black music. Although not religious (but having its **roots** in spirituals and gospel singing), soul has been used as an adjective as well as a noun. For example, "Rhythm and Blues," the black forerunner **and** contemporary counterpart of "Rock 'n' Roll" would be said to have had "soul," but was not soul as a style. (*Soul as a style* being the chronological parallel of Rock.) Among the more famous stars of soul have been The Temptations, James Brown, The Supremes, Aretha Franklin and Stevie Wonder.

Jazz-Rock. The style of jazz-rock can be thought of as rock which incorporated elements of a "jazz-style" improvisation; it also refers to jazz which began using rock beats. Early in "jazz-rock," rock-oriented groups (using jazz-style improvisation) forged the style (groups such as Blood, Sweat and Tears); later jazz-rock groups and individual performers came from the jazz field or had been equally versed in both styles—groups and individuals such as Chicago, Buddy Rich, Herbie Mann, and Quincy Jones.

Folk-Rock. A hybrid of soft-rock with folklike melodies, from American Folk Music (as songs by folk singers such as Woodie Guthrie, Burl Ives, Pete Seeger, Peter, Paul, and Mary). Folk-rock is illustrated by some of the recordings of Bob Dylan, Joan Baez, Judy Collins, or Joni Mitchell. Folk-rock has used amplified guitars (whereas the purists insisted upon accoustical guitars). The rock beats used in folk-rock are not used in so-called **pure** folk music.

Country and Western. The style of "Country and Western" always enjoyed huge popularity in large areas of the country; urban areas only had a keyhole glimpse of this style, through radio and T.V. programs such as *The Grand Ole Opry,* or Gene Autrey and Roy Rogers movies. In the late 1960s and 1970s, country singers such as Tennessee Ernie Ford, Johnny Cash, Charley Pride, and Merl Haggard gained greater prominence. Glenn Cambell further popularized the style with songs such as "By the Time I Get to Phoenix," "Wichita Lineman," and "Rhinestone Cowboy." The country guitar used is sometimes different from amplified guitars used in pop music or rock (occasionally rock and pop use the country guitar); and in country music, violins are used in the specific "country style" of playing. Lyrics in country music often deal with obscure situations often overlooked in pop music—such as a truck driver's driving over a specific highway. In country music, lyrics often are framed uniquely as in the phrase, "I've erased you from the blackboard of my heart." Just as "swing" used to be **the** popular style of the big cities, there are many parts of the country where "Country and Western was **the** popular music of the 1950s, 1960s, **and** 1970s.

New Calypso or Regge. New Calypso or Regge—including the dance "The Hustle"—is a style many West Indian students relate to well. (This is why it should be included in Side 1, especially if many Jamaicans, Trinidadians, or students from Barbados are in a class.) Every several years, new beats from the Caribbean permeate popular music, as do rhythms from Hi-Life Music of West Africa. New Calypso beats enjoyed great popularity in the middle 1970s.

The Steel Drum

ROCK MY SOUL

Gospel. Most spirituals were originally sung unaccompanied since the slaves had no instruments. Modern gospel music, on the other hand, usually uses a keyboard instrument as an accompaniment. Although most gospel songs have been composed by one person, many have been passed down from generation to generation in the folk tradition. Among the more famous, "He's Got the Whole World in His Hands," was originally a spiritual. (Many Baptist Churches will help you obtain gospel music.)

HE'S GOT THE WHOLE WORLD IN HIS HANDS

Bluegrass. The term "bluegrass" did not achieve very widespread usage, really, until the late 1960s. It refers to an attempt to restore some of the purity to mountain music of the Blue Ridge area. (Check record listings for specific artists labeled as bluegrass, such as, Bill Monroe and the Bluegrass Boys, Earl Scruggs, Jimmy Martin, or the Stanley Brothers.)

United States Western or Cowboy Songs. Anyone who grew up with the sounds of Roy Rogers or Gene Autrey, in frequent movie hits, knows the sound referred to by the term "Western." (In the late 1960s and early '70s Johnny Cash became a favorite performer with "Country and Western" songs which are different from "Cowboy Western.") Among the classics of "Cowboy or Western" songs are those like "Tumblin' Tumbleweed," "Don't Fence Me In," "Cool Water," or "Jesse James." You might prefer to call them cowboy songs. Cowboy songs that are even older are "On Top of Old Smokey," "Old Chisholm Trail," or "Streets of Laredo."

OLD SMOKY

OLD CHISHOLM TRAIL

STREETS OF LAREDO

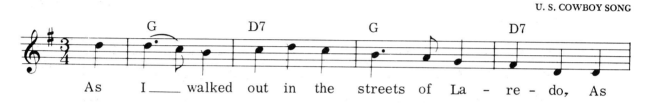

RED RIVER VALLEY

Revolutionary War Songs. Some songs of the American Revolution have become well known. Among the most famous is "Chester," a hymn composed by William Billings in 1770, but sung as a marching song by the Continental Army. Of course, there is also "Yankee Doodle," which is well known and the most popular.

YANKEE DOODLE

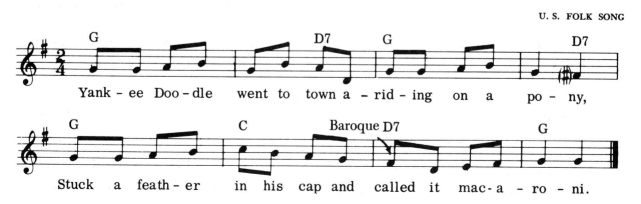

Civil War Songs. Songs from the Civil War have attained popularity. "When Johnny Comes Marching Home" was actually composed by Patrick Gilmore (1829-1892) but is looked upon as sort of a Civil War folk song. Others that are truly *traditional* in the sense that the composers are unknown are "Oh Freedom," "We Are Marching on to Victory," and "The Abolitionist Hymn." "John Brown's Body," the tune of which was later used for Julia Ward Howe's "Battle Hymn of the Republic," used music said to be written by William Steffe.

WHEN JOHNNY COMES MARCHING HOME

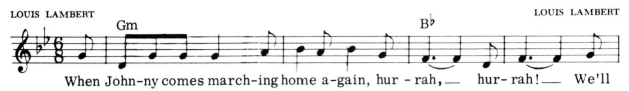

BATTLE HYMN OF THE REPUBLIC

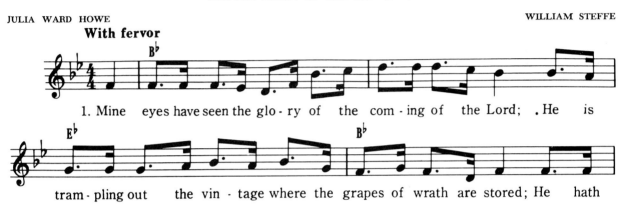

White Spirituals. The term White Spiritual was sometimes used for white songs that also expressed hope that someday hard times will disappear and oppression will end. Included in the category are "Goin' Down the Road" and "Life Is a Toil."

GOIN' DOWN THE ROAD

Sea Chanties. Sea chanties are folk songs almost always listed as "Anon," meaning traditional or of unknown origin. Among those that can be found easily are the American Chanty "Blow the Man Down."

BLOW YE WINDS

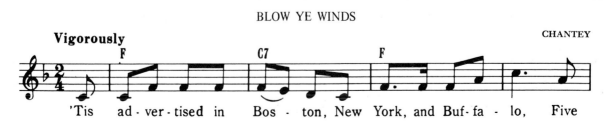

Songs From the British Isles (Ireland, Wales, and Scotland). The most famous Welsh folk song, perhaps, is "All Through the Night." Among famous Scotch songs are "Loch Lomond," "Bluebells of Scotland," or "Auld Lang Syne." English folk songs include "Greensleeves" and "Drink to Me Only with Thine Eyes." Irish folk songs are so well known that you might try one a little different such as "Gypsy Rover." (If the familiar is preferred use "Danny Boy.")

ALL THROUGH THE NIGHT

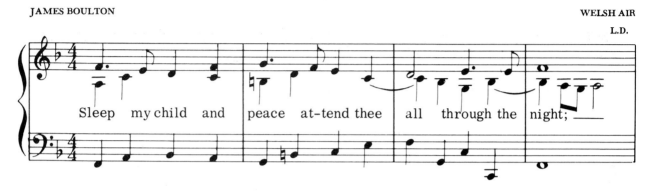

LOCH LOMOND

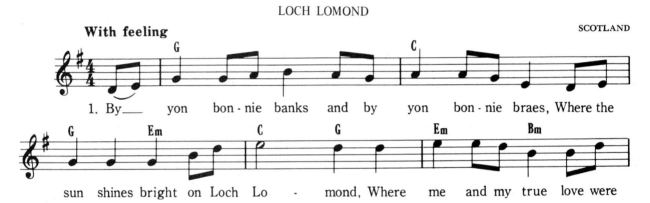

GREENSLEEVES

Other European Folk Songs. French folk songs have often been used in schools (*Aupres de ma Blonde* or the popular round *Frere Jacques,* ["Are You Sleeping"]). *Ach, Du Lieber Augustin* is probably the most widely used German folk song. Russian folk songs are exciting and usually liked by children (see if you can find *Korobushka* or *Minka*). Among the "catchy" Spanish folk songs are *El Vito* and *La Sinda.* The Netherlands, Italy, Czechoslovakia, and Poland have also generated many well-known folk songs (that can be found easily in recordings or in books of folk songs).

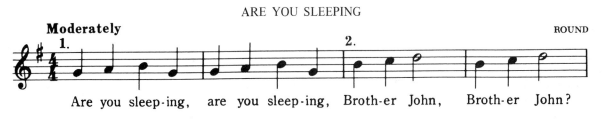

Oriental (Chinese and Japanese). Some Chinese and Japanese folk songs are of the utmost and rare beauty; such is the case with the Chinese folk songs "The Flower of China," "Crescent Moon," and *Feng Yang Song** and the Japanese folk songs *Usagi, Usagi* ("Rabbit in the Moon"), *Hiraita, Hiraita* ("Flowers Blossom and Close"), and *Hitori De Sabishii* ("Alone and Sad").**

LIGHT CLASSICAL *(Side 4)*

Light classical music is an excellent transition from popular music to the classics of composers such as Mozart, Bach, and Beethoven. Often, light classical music is neglected by those overly zealous to change taste and "convert the heathens." Light classical music is an effective bridge because large orchestras or sophisticated orchestrations are used, but with an eye to popular appeal.

Sousa Marches. It may be almost a *cliche* to say everyone loves John Philip Sousa Marches; but it is probably true. You can use the universally known "Stars and Stripes" or the well-known "Washington Post March."

Overtures. Children will react immediately to the *William Tell Overture,* written by Rossini, especially when

Gioachino Rossini

*Lawrence Eisman, Elizabeth Jones, and Raymond Malone, *Making Music Your Own* (Morristown: Silver Burdett Company, 1971).
**Donald Paul Berger, *Folk Songs of Japanese Children* (Tokyo: Charles E. Tuttle Co., 1969).

they hear the portion that was used for "The Lone Ranger." Both the *Poet and the Peasant* and the *Light Cavalry Overture* should also elicit strong responses from children. You can also use overtures to Gilbert and Sullivan operettas or the very lilting overture to *The Merry Widow.*

Operettas. In addition to opera overtures, portions of operettas can be used. "Three Little Maids from School" from Gilbert and Sullivan's *The Mikado,* or "Never Never Sick at Sea" from *H.M.S. Pinafore,* make delightful listening for children. (Children often resist opera when first exposed to it, because most operas are in a foreign language and opera uses what they sometimes laughingly think of as shrieking. Therefore, broadway musicals or operettas in English serve as an important transition from popular music to the world of opera.) *The Merry Widow* is a delightful operetta that children always enjoy, especially if it is performed in English.

Comic Operas. Children often ask "What is the difference between an operetta and a comic opera?" The answers are not always clear or even correct. Many comic operas have spoken dialogue, as in operettas (and had not comic operas existed before the term *operetta* was used, any comic operas could have been called operettas). Perhaps the most famous comic opera is Rossini's *The Barber of Seville.* ("Largo al factorum" is the most famous comic aria from this comic opera.) In recent years, Gian Carlo Menotti wrote comic operas with popular appeal, such as *The Telephone.* (Menotti's *The Medium* is fascinating to children even though it is a serious rather than comic opera.)

Strauss Waltzes and Polkas. The use of the full orchestra, in this style of music with immediate appeal, makes it another excellent bridge to classical music. (Johann Strauss was the most famous composer of waltzes, but there were other Strausses and other excellent composers.) Children can be encouraged to dance when listening to waltzes and polkas. By the way, Strauss rhymes with mouse, and he also wrote a famous operetta *Die Fledermaus.*

Johann Strauss

Tangos and Zarzuelas. The Argentine tango (made famous in America in Rudolf Valentino movies) combined a dance *and* an art form. It is another excellent bridge between popular and classical music because of using the full orchestra. Spanish *Zarzuelas* (pronounced "tharthuales"), light operas from Spain, are also an excellent transition from music of popular appeal to the classics (especially the overtures).

Castenets

CLASSICAL (*Side 5*)

At this point, you might think it more difficult (and correctly so) to create original introductions to classical music you've chosen. However, the task is easier with the help of the record jackets or with a brief but accurate reference such as the *Harvard Brief Dictionary of Music.** You may or may not want to refer historically to the times in which the music was created. (See pages 36-39.)

Classical excerpts should be brief; emphasis should be upon identification and comparison of sounds; brevity will minimize negative reactions by students.

Below are categories of musical styles, with some specific suggestions for compositions to choose. Prepare your introduction in writing; *don't mispronounce names on the tape; and be sure you have the correct composition that you're introducing on the cassette.*

Renaissance. Choose music by Palestrina, Ockeghem, or Lassus (DiLasso); they are composers frequently cited as representative of the Renaissance. (You might compare their music with Gregorian Chants of the Medieval period.)

Baroque. Choose and discuss Vivaldi's *Four Seasons;* and anything by Bach and Handel. Handel's *Waterworks* or The *Messiah* are fine; Bach's *Brandenburg Concertos* can be used, or popularized versions of his works such as those done by the Swingle Singers or on the recording "Switched on Bach."

Viennese Classical. For Viennese classicism, Mozart's *G Minor Symphony* is frequently used; but students often enjoy more hearing and discussing Haydn's *Surprise Symphony* or *Clock Symphony.* (See photographs in Chapter One, page 38.)

Romanticism. The spirit of Romanticism is captured in Beethoven's *Pastoral* (Sixth), and Third or *Eroica Symphony*—although Beethoven's *Fifth Symphony* and *Ninth Symphony* are more famous. Often played (as capturing the romantic spirit) is Schubert's so-called *Unfinished Symphony.* Late romanticism, with its grand nationalism, is embodied in such works as the *1812 Overture* by Tchaikowsky (Chi-Kov-skee) and the overture to *Die Meistersinger* by Wagner (Vahgner). (See Chapter One, page 38.)

Vivaldi

Johannas Ockeghem
with Chapel Singers

Chopin

Impressionism. Delius's *Florida Suite* or *Afternoon of a Faun* by Debussy (Deb-you-see) or Ravel's *Bolero* can be used. For post-impressionism you can use the popular *Grand Canyon Suite* by Ferde Grofe.

*Willi Apel and Ralph T. Daniel (eds.), *The Harvard Brief Dictionary of Music* (New York: Washington Square Press, 1966).

Debussy

Ravel

Barbarism. *Allegro Barbaro* by Bartok or Stravinsky's *Rite of Spring.* (Post-Barbarism: music from *Jaws.*)

Expressionism. The "Dance of the Seven Veils" by Richard (Ri-Kard) Strauss; or music by Schoenberg (Shern-berg) such as *Verklarte Nacht* (Ver-Klair-ta Nacht).

Neo-Classicism. Prokofiev's *Classical Symphony.* Stravinsky's *Pulcinella Suite.*

Electronic and Musique Concrète. In recent years many excellent recordings of electronic music have come out; choose anything by Luening, Ussechevsky, Babbitt, or Mimaruglu.

Aleatory and Chance. Discuss John Cage's *4'33"* as nothing but silence in which you listen for the sounds you hear around you. (Record the sounds heard when attempting to "perform" this composition.)

Bartok

Stravinsky

Serge Prokofiev

Arnold Schoenberg

CHAPTER THREE

Toward Becoming the School Music Specialist

Concept: It is not exceedingly difficult to be in charge of school musical plays and talent shows, or even to start a band or chorus; but some additional insights are needed for you to be considered the school music specialist.

In times of economic stress, budgetary cuts eliminate certified specialists in many fields including music. Therefore, a classroom teacher has the opportunity of developing a music specialty which can be used in situations involving the need for added music skills. One who already plays the piano or guitar, of course, is often preferred; but you can make yourself "in demand" by engaging in some of the activities listed below.

STAGING PLAYS AND MUSICALS IN THE ASSEMBLY

It is easiest to start with a nonmusical play. After you have successfully staged one or more you can expand into staging a musical; below are different ways to go about this.

Using Recordings. One way to do a musical play is by using recordings in the background. Actually it is best to rerecord the records onto tape, just in case the recordings are lost or broken (or the phonograph doesn't work); then you have *two* alternatives. When using recordings or tape, the performers in the play "sing along" with the records.

Using an Accompanist. You can use a student or a teacher as an accompanist. But if you use a student (no matter how good), the music must be less complex. If you find a teacher who plays the piano or guitar, of course it is preferable. For some of the rock musicals a guitar can be used. In **all** of the above instances, of course, more rehearsing is needed than when using recordings. (Recordings can be turned up to compensate for students who "go-off" rhythm and sing off-tune; but if possible it is preferable to eliminate use of recordings as a crutch, and try for a "live-music" situation, in which the accompanist is leading **and** following the singer.)

STAGING TALENT SHOWS

If a Building Principal approves the staging of a talent show, and you do a good job, this is another way of working towards being a music or talent resource person.

Scheduling Auditions. A first step in staging a talent show is scheduling auditions. To get widest publicity, rexograph, or send mimeographed notices home to parents; but usually it is unnecessary, as the word spreads rapidly that there is going to be a talent show (and that students will be allowed to audition for the teacher in charge). If you schedule auditions during lunch, you may have to miss part of your lunch period; but this is the least complicated solution. It merely involves taking one or several children up at a time from the lunchroom. As a second alternative, students can be taken out of other rooms *with teachers' permission* during your free periods; occasionally, however, teachers complain that students miss work (unless you take them during a physical education period). A third way involves auditioning students before school; even if the principal approves, however, you must get parent-permission slips for children to come to school early. The same applies if you want to audition students after school. A fourth way, to audition students for a talent show, is for a teacher to bring an entire class to you (in your room or the auditorium). In some respects this is the least desirable alternative; but some teachers may not cooperate any other way.

Organizing the Talent Show. After you have chosen the students whom you feel have the most talent, you must choose a format, and decide whether you will use a student announcer or do the announcing yourself. Beginning teachers sometimes let students do too much. Try to limit each student or group to one or two numbers at most. If using a student announcer, a simple but effective script must be written.

PLANNING DANCE AND SPECIAL EVENTS PROGRAMS

Halloween. Halloween assemblies or programs are always fun, with witches, goblins, pumpkins, black cats, and ghosts. Among music that can be used is *Dance Macabre* by Saint-Saens.

Columbus Day. Columbus Day is another holiday that can be the subject for an auditorium play with music. For a change, try composing an **original** song involving Queen Isabella (or the Nina, Pinta, and Santa Maria).

Thanksgiving. Who does not get pleasure out of seeing elementary school children going to school dressed for a Thanksgiving play? Costumes of pilgrims, turkey pictures, Indian Corn props, and pumpkin pie are all part of the fun. Among songs that can be sung in the presentation are "Come Ye Thankful People" and "Prayer of Thanksgiving"; of course, students can dance to "Turkey in the Straw."

COME, YE THANKFUL PEOPLE, COME

HENRY ALFORD   GEORGE J. ELVEY

PRAYER OF THANKSGIVING

THEODORE BAKER   NETHERLANDS HYMN

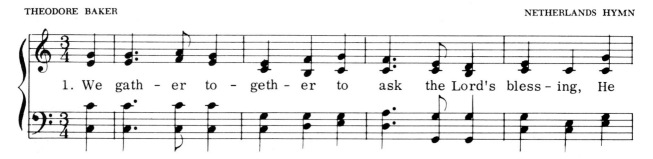

Christmas and Chanukah. Few schools do nothing for Christmas and Chanukah. If you wish to become a school music specialist, and you have not chosen to plan a talent show or a play that included music for Halloween, Columbus Day, or Thanksgiving, Christmas and Chanukah affords much opportunity. Song material is well known and can even be sung *a capella*—certainly with resonator bells or autoharp if you don't play the piano or guitar well enough (or won't be able to get a student or teacher accompanist).

THE TWELVE DAYS OF CHRISTMAS

SILENT NIGHT

JOSEPH MOHR   FRANZ GRUBER

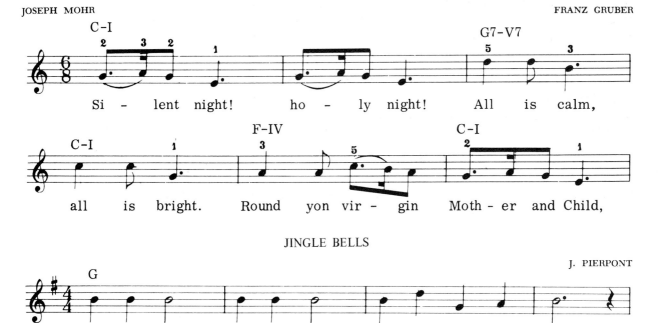

Si - lent night! ho - ly night! All is calm,

all is bright. Round yon vir - gin Moth - er and Child,

JINGLE BELLS

J. PIERPONT

Jin - gle bells, jin - gle bells, jin - gle all the way.

Ethnic Assemblies. Increasingly, special assemblies are being staged that involve song and dance from a variety of cultures represented in a school. Some of the larger "minority groups" are Italian, Chinese, Japanese, Korean, Greek, American Indian, Polish, Jewish, Black (including West Indian and Haitian), and Hispanic (including Puerto Rican, Mexican, and Cuban). Recently, Black Solidarity Day is an appropriate holiday and theme; Latin American Week is another; French Week is another. Often, assemblies can be planned for these occasions that are colorful and entertaining. With these in mind, you can use your imagination and originate an assembly program that will make you a strong contender for the role of a music specialist.

EVERYBODY LOVES SATURDAY NIGHT

Key: D Major

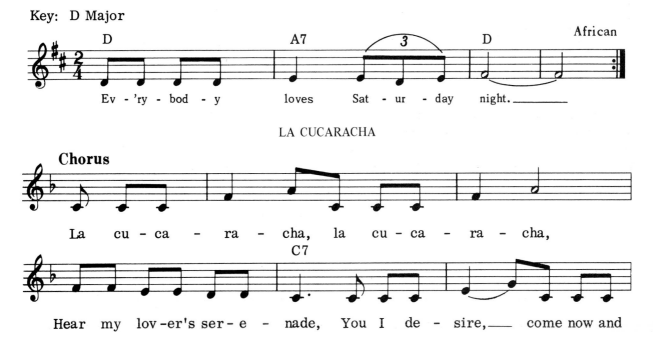

Ev - 'ry - bod - y loves Sat - ur - day night._____

LA CUCARACHA

La cu - ca - ra - cha, la cu - ca - ra - cha,

Hear my lov-er's ser-e - nade, You I de - sire,___ come now and

United Nations Day. Programs planned for United Nations Day can be similar to "Ethnic Assemblies" (except they needn't involve cultures only represented by the students in the school). Diverse cultures can be spotlighted: Eskimo, African, Indian, Polynesian, Finnish. You will probably have to use recorded music although with some research and rehearsing you can teach students to sing songs from faraway lands.

KUMBAYA

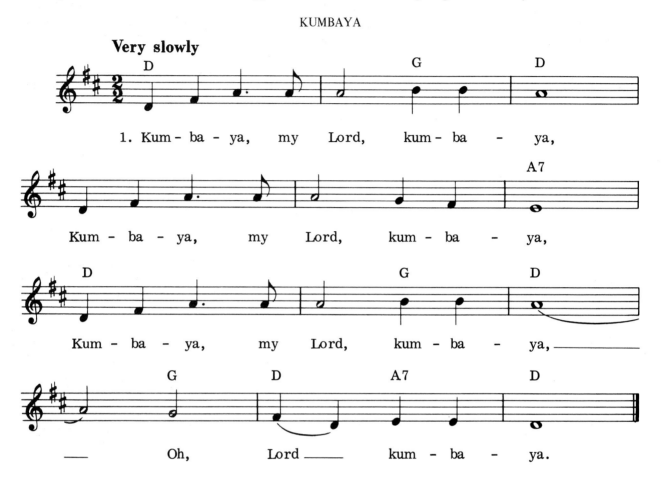

AUDITORIUM SINGS

Auditorium sings are different from a special assembly program in that they involve the *entire* auditorium rather than a few on stage. In many ways this is harder, but below are suggestions for making the task easier.

Using Filmstrips. Filmstrip and record sets are available, so you need only flash words to songs on a screen and play a recording with which students will "sing-along." Sometimes motivation is a problem; but motivation often depends upon which filmstrips are chosen. None are suggested here, because the filmstrip and record set should be "tailor-made" and chosen for the specific student body. Be sure to preview the filmstrips so you can try to motivate good participation; but prepare for some failures anyway; use the filmstrip and record set only for 10-15 minutes the first time you do this; possibly consider giving special rewards to the classes that participate best in an auditorium sing.

Using Pop Recordings. Use of popular recordings is no longer frowned upon in music education; thus you can capitalize upon student interest in the "now music" for auditorium sings. Most students want to listen to "top 40" music and many *will* sing along with them. If possible, obtain the current sheet music for the latest songs and make a transparency that can be projected onto an overhead screen. (Consider establishing some friendly competition between classes or between boys and girls.)

Transparencies or Songsheets Plus an Accompanist. Once having successfully used a filmstrip or certain popular recordings, you might challenge an auditorium to sing without the "crutch" of the recording. This would work best if your piano playing is satisfactory, or if you have the benefit of a good teacher (or student) accompanist.

STARTING A CHORUS

Among the important aspects of starting a chorus are repertory (the songs you will sing) and announcing auditions. In addition, you should have a general idea of voice placement, and whether you will use boys and girls in the chorus or just girls.

Auditions. Auditions create interest and excitement. Selectivity makes students want to be in a performing group even more. By not accepting some students, the chorus takes on greater prestige. Auditions can take place during lunch or before or after school if you have both the Principal's and the parents' permission. You can also send for students while you have a prep period. (See page 53 on auditions.)

Testing Voices. Voice testing need not be a terrifying ordeal. Students can either sing "My Country 'tis of Thee" (properly called *America*); "America the Beautiful"; "The Star Spangled Banner"; or a song of their choice. (*Bashful students should be permitted to sing into a cassette tape recorder.*) Students should also be able to "match pitches" that you play on the piano, guitar, or bells.

AMERICA

AMERICA THE BEAUTIFUL

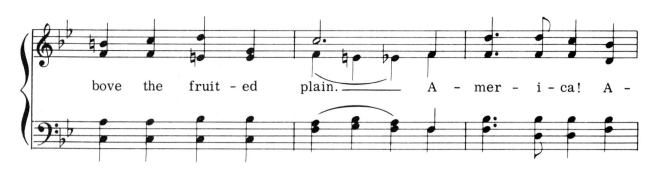

bove   the   fruit - ed   plain. _____   A - mer - i - ca!   A -

THE STAR-SPANGLED BANNER

FRANCIS SCOTT KEY   JOHN STAFFORD SMITH

1. O   say!   can   you   see,   by   the   dawn's ear-ly   light, What   so

proud - ly   we   hailed   at   the   twi - light's last   gleam-ing? Whose broad

stripes   and   bright   stars,   thro'   the   per - il - ous   fight,   O'er   the

ram - parts   we   watch'd, were   so   gal-lant-ly   stream-ing!   And the

rock - ets' red   glare,   the   bombs   burst-ing   in   air,   Gave

proof   thro'   the   night —   that   our   flag   was   still   there.

Chorus

O   say, does that —   Star-Span-gled   Ban - ner —   yet —   wave —   O'er the

land ———   of the   free   and the   home   of the   brave?

Motivating Students to Be in Harmony Sections. It is difficult to get boys in the chorus, and difficult to get students to sing harmony parts rather than "the tune." Among the ways students can be coaxed gently into harmonizing are techniques offering both extrinsic and intrinsic rewards. A "harmony group" may be excused from regular classes *more* than the group that sings melody; or students can be shown through recordings how important harmony groups are; if necessary a harmony group can receive preferential treatment (or even go on a trip if persuasion is badly needed).

Using an Accompanist. A good accompanist is necessary when starting a chorus, and trying to recruit members. If you cannot play well, or cannot get a teacher who plays well, perhaps a parent or a community piano teacher might agree to accompany the school chorus. Eventually a budget might permit paying a small sum to an accompanist.

Using a Guitar and Other Easy-to-Play Instruments. For many types of songs a guitar sounds even better than a piano as an accompanying instrument. The guitar is even easier to play than is commonly thought; but if you don't play one, it is fairly certain that one of the teachers in the school will—the problem will be to persuade that teacher to serve the school by being an accompanist for the chorus (usually, the person is *sure* that his or her level of performance is *not* adequate for real application). You might also find that, for some songs, the autoharp is perfectly adequate. Look for books containing songs that use three chords or less (songs such as "Water Come to My Eye," "Skip to My Lou," "Red River Valley," or *Alouette*). Songs also exist which can be performed with great effect with easy-to-play instruments other than the guitar or autoharp: "Silent Night" sounds very effective with resonator bells alone; "The Donkey Serenade" sounds effective with only a conga and maracas.

Maracas

ALOUETTE

FRENCH-CANADIAN FOLK SONG

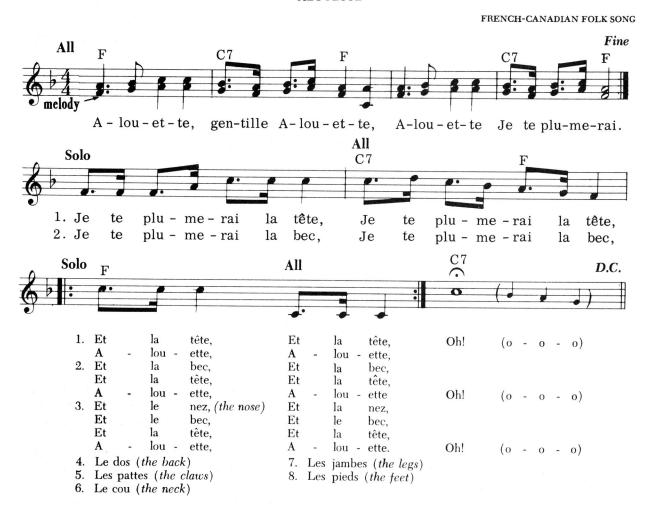

	1.	Et	la	tête,	Et	la	tête,	Oh!	(o - o - o)
		A - lou - ette,		A - lou - ette,					
	2.	Et	la	bec,	Et	la	bec,		
		Et	la	tête,	Et	la	tête,		
		A - lou - ette,		A - lou - ette			Oh!	(o - o - o)
	3.	Et	le	nez, *(the nose)*	Et	la	nez,		
		Et	le	bec,	Et	le	bec,		
		Et	la	tête,	Et	la	tête,		
		A - lou - ette,		A - lou - ette.			Oh!	(o - o - o)

4. Le dos (*the back*)   7. Les jambes (*the legs*)
5. Les pattes (*the claws*)   8. Les pieds (*the feet*)
6. Le cou (*the neck*)

Note: To make this an action fun song, have the class point to the parts of the body corresponding to those mentioned in the song.

STARTING A BAND

The initial organization of a band should include knowing the following: (1) what type of music you want to play; (2) what instruments you can deal with; and (3) what instruments you can order with the money you have. For example, if you don't have a broad musical background but used to play the trumpet, you should consider starting with only trumpets and drums. If you play the piano well but know *nothing* about "transposition," you might consider starting with only nontransposing instruments such as flutes and assorted bells (melode, resonator, and lyra). Leave funds for music stands and music—don't spend all your money on instruments. Finally, obtain *several* manuals rather than one on teaching the fingerings and how to blow various instruments; **don't** rely on just one.

Auditions. Auditions and selectivity should be used to create excitement. Selectivity will also eliminate students whose behavior may impede the group's progress during the difficult first weeks of getting started.

What if you want to start a band but have *no* instruments? Then the role of auditions is clear—you need students who have their own instruments **and** are willing to bring them to school. (Unfortunately, you may get five drummers, four electric guitar players, and five electric bass players. This situation not only would be difficult to manage, but would also present a security problem. You might have to drive students to, and home from, school. And, it would require a secure area for storage with at least a double-lock scheme.)

In addition, everything said about auditions for a chorus is applicable here. The reader should consult pages 57-60.

Ordering Instruments. Because prices change, specific recommendations cannot be given on how to spend specific sums. Where there are limited funds, it is wise to remember that students gravitate toward percussion instruments, electric guitars, and electric bass (and, although formal training is needed to play them well, often good results can be obtained with high motivation alone). Also, remember that the less experienced one is in teaching diverse instruments, the more important it is to group instruments homogeneously. That means, for example, that if you don't play many instruments of the orchestra, it will be better for you to order and teach ten clarinets than ten assorted instruments.

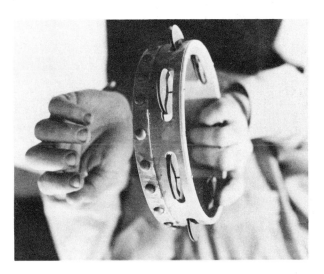

Tambourine

Regarding percussion instruments, inner-city students will take great delight in forming a rock, pop, soul, or Latin band that includes a conga, bongos, timbales, a cowbell, tambourine, maracas, guiro, claves, and/or a full "trap-set" (dance band drums). For urban situations, therefore, these instruments are particularly recommended, and should be ordered. (See Chapter One pp. 31-34.)

A problem with an all-percussion band is the volume of noise. It is not recommended that percussion instruments be ordered in large numbers, if there is no classroom or auditorium out of the way and noise proof. A noise-proof auditorium is particularly helpful.

As previously stated, if a homogeneous group of instruments is decided upon, start ordering instruments that you may have played when you were a child. Or, if you have *no* background in instruments such as the clarinet, trumpet, trombone, or saxophone, consider a small band using assorted bells: melode bells, lyras, resonator bells, and glockenspiel. Younger students (third and fourth grade) will offer no resistance; upper graders (fifth and sixth grade) might complain that they want to play trumpets, saxophones, and guitars. While you work with a group of bell players, remember too that you *might* come across students who play their own instruments well enough so that all you have to do is give them the music you want to play. (See Chapter One, pp. 28-29.)

Choosing Repertory. With limited experience, a beginning band can be used in one of two ways: (1) as an aid to the chorus—playing harmony or background, or the melody "in unison"; (2) as an interpreter of popular songs—in which case students will be highly motivated to practice and perform.

Using an Accompanist. In the early stages of forming a band, an accompanist may be particularly important—especially if your band members only play a few notes (and you need to put on a performance). In that case, try to play something that does indeed use only a few notes, yet is rhythmically exciting—*the accompanist doing something fancier and more impressive!* The net result will be "wow, what a job in only several months!" Use tunes such as "Jingle Bells," a single note "riff," or television and movie themes that use a limited number of notes.

MUSIC IN SPECIAL EDUCATION

Music should be included in any curriculum for special education classes—whether they be intellectually gifted, educable mentally retarded, or disabled.

Teaching the Intellectually Gifted. Without experience, one may think that some of the information (and concepts) presented are beyond the scope of the average child. But, average youngsters can comprehend much of what has been presented in some way.* However, the gifted child can be challenged even further; the gifted child is even more capable of being challenged with analytical and historical approaches to music. Some children may not comprehend analogies between the history of the Renaissance and Palestrina's music; but gifted students may enjoy the challenge of writing a report on the relationships between the *Pope Marcellus Mass* (by Palestrina) and The Last Supper (by DaVinci).

A music specialist, in a school, might play a very important role in the school's special education curriculum (if there is one). This might take the form of music history for the intellectually gifted, or giving the gifted a leadership role in the school's chorus or orchestra.

The Educable Mentally Retarded. In inner-city schools, the largest special education group is the educable mentally retarded. Yet, too often, they are not included in school music activities. (This is especially true if the school is geared to competitive performances of their band and/or chorus.) The retarded should be permitted to explore every phase of music. Because of limited conceptual development, some types of progress may be slow—such as the reading and writing of music. But, performance on (and interest in) the easy-to-play instruments may be excellent.

Children who are labeled "CRMD" or "educable mentally retarded" often show a very strong drive in the direction of music. For this reason, music should be included in their daily activities. As one experienced teacher of CRMD classes wrote:

Music must be woven into the very fabric of each day. A CRMD child grows through music as he becomes a participant to some degree in every phase of the program. In a good program, music becomes a part of the child's life, a part of the child's day, and a support to other areas of learning. The music program generates a love and appreciation of music, through music experiences and participation in music activities.

Many nonverbal approaches must be used with youngsters who are slow learners. These same nonverbal approaches have considerable applicability to working with regular classes, or to working with bilingual students. Thus, the experience of working with the educable mentally retarded can be important and useful, as well as rewarding.

Another important aspect of working with the educable mentally retarded is that a lesson must be reduced to its smallest component parts. This can have considerable application to lessons with "difficult" classes—those in which there are disciplinary problems. It is important that a teacher know how to get across a single idea, before disruptive students distract the students who are trying to concentrate.

The fact that a whole note will get four beats, in 4/4 meter, may only be part of a lesson with a bright, well-behaved class. But the same lesson may be too long and abstract—if done in its entirety—for either retarded or disruptive students. For that reason, teachers should learn how to communicate and drill small pieces of information, as well as how to break down and incorporate an idea.

*See Jerome S. Bruner, *The Process of Education* (New York: Vintage Books, 1960).

Disabled or Blind Students. When attending a local elementary school, blind or disabled children also have a right to the pleasures derived from music. Much of the complexity that we assume to be "over the heads" of normal children, moreover, *can* be dealt with—when students have increased motivation, because of being handicapped. Just as art may have greater meaning to a child who is deaf, music may have greater meaning to a child who is blind. (Braille was originally invented to enable the blind to read music.)

Although the disabled may not be able to play many instruments, there are many instruments that can be substituted for children who cannot use their (or have artificial) limbs. The harmonica or mouth organ is one that is particularly helpful—especially if it is mounted, so that it need not be held.

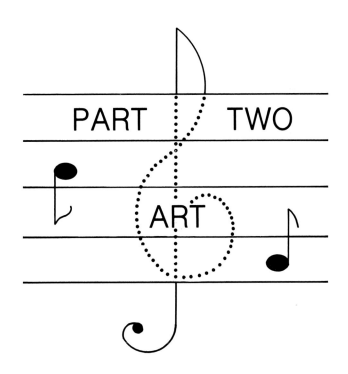

PART TWO

Art Teaching in an Urban Setting

The urban teacher of art encounters a wide range of students. One may work with students of various social levels, cultures, and experiences. The urban art room is representative of the urban community bringing together children of various abilities. The excitement in urban art teaching, as well as its difficulties, have the same derivation; both depend upon working with children who have a wide range of ability, attitudes, and exposures to art. The diversity allows for a variety of interpretations and responses to art problems posed by the teacher.

The urban art teacher may work in art rooms of the most advanced design, or in a multipurpose class designed for reading, writing, and listening—(into which is pushed "the art-cart" containing paper and crayons). In one school, the teacher may be called the "artist in residence," or a "specialist." In another, she will be the classroom teacher with multiple functions including the teaching of art. In some elementary schools, the art teacher may be one of a team of subject matter specialists or may be responsible for carrying forth the message of art ("single-handed ") to an entire school. In certain schools the art teacher may have the support of the administration in their belief in the values of art. In other situations, it is a matter of covering classroom teachers during their preparation periods. In most instances, art experiences in the school heavily depend on the resourcefulness, creativity, and enthusiasm of the individual art teacher. Students in the art class will be there for a variety of reasons. Some may have been diagnosed as talented. Other students may have been unsuccessful in meeting the verbal and academic demands of the school and be considered as "problem" cases.

In spite of the above *categorized diversities,* there are several *commonalities* on which the urban art program can be based. They involve the experiences of the city itself; its multisensory phenomena including its sounds, forms, colors, themes, and movements which both the teacher and child have in common. The *visual language* of the city is also characterized by the child's involvement with media. In this part of the book, actual examples of student artwork are used to illustrate these concepts.

CHAPTER FOUR

Art Education in the City

Concept: The city is the home of the artist. It is a man-made environment designed in all its aspects by an assortment of visual artists. The city acts as a showcase for the artist's work both in its formal institutions—the museums and galleries, and its informal exhibits of fashion, billboards, and traffic signs. It is an up-to-date exhibit of all the contemporary arts contrasted with historic antecedents in a combined setting. The artists who continuously create and re-create the city draw their energies and inspirations from the city and return their contributions to it. Art education must consider its status as a city art.

THE CITY AS A WORK OF ART

The city displays its artists in a natural totality. One can sense a feeling of past, present, and future, the sensation of change and evolution. A contemporary piece of sculpture may sprawl in front of a federal-style building which displays examples of graphic illustrations. Living in the city means having continuous contact with visual forms and objects; also viewing, wearing, and selecting the products of visual artists.

For school art to benefit from the interest of its setting, it has to place itself in the midst of its environment. Most school art experiences should begin by observation, reaction, and selection from the environment. Its materials and forms are derived from city life. People in the city continuously interact with artists and their products. This interaction may occur through the arrangement and display of objects in a store, by parking one's car, by painting one's fence, or by stacking one's garbage bags. The people in the city continuously interact with the artist when they select consumer goods, choose places to live, or pick films to see.

Art education has to slow down the city pace so that one can focus on the details. The enormous complexity of the city often distorts our functional vision and disallows 'seeing'. Art has to enlarge on the theme of interaction with the city, providing experiences in aesthetic selection and arrangement; it not only has to use the city as a model, but should afford the opportunity to remake it. Art education may become congruous with the city principles of form, scale, and movement. But, it cannot be dwarfed by its size.

The city often makes its viewers feel helpless. In art education, the child is to be afforded the opportunity to remake his vision of the city, thereby gaining the understanding of its grids, systems, and geometry. The child is permitted to gain a sense of understanding, power, and control. In using the city model as a basis of art education, many artificial barriers are removed between the visual artists, as well as barriers between art communicated by the artist and the nonartist; between visual phenomena that are accidental and those which are purposeful. Thus, the maker of art is brought closer to the consumer of art.

Food packages, for example, which are products of *packaging artists* are stacked into "sculptural forms" by the supermarket clerk (to be selected by the consumer both for content and aethetic appeal of the box).

The study of city art has to do with materials both old and new, many originally shaped by an artist and reshaped by its user. A car that was the product of an industrial designer may be altered by its dents and cracks—thus it is further reshaped by its owner.

While artists have traditionally reacted to nature and the human form for inspiration, a "city artist" consults other city artists and their ideas. School art, therefore, has to involve itself with the understanding of the works of all the visual artists whose works make up the city.

Formal Archives of Art. The urban environment is the center of art collecting and art exhibiting. Museums, galleries, and private collections form elaborate networks of displays. The museums provide art classes (for teachers, students, and parents), exhibition guides, and lectures in areas of specific interest. Museums often house children's galleries, exhibiting artworks of special interest to children. The museum shops, library, and media loan centers are resources available to art teachers. Museums reach out to the community providing artworks on loan, speakers, and consultants to school programs.

Art galleries showcase the latest in contemporary works. Gallery exhibits are often dedicated to the recent works of a single artist; the exhibit, a series, or sequence of a single idea.

Cultural, historical, and industrial museums not specifically dedicated to the fine arts are often excellent resources to urban forms of the past and present. Libraries may be considered as centers for visual research. The artist looks through books and reproductions in reference to his work. The libraries of art schools, in particular, are excellent sources for reproductions and other visuals.

Less formal places where art education may turn for resources in the city include automobile showrooms for the study of industrial design, department stores to develop awareness of trends in fashion, pottery shops to see handcrafts, or perhaps bakeries for food design. The antique store and flea market, a popular phenomenon in the city, is an excellent source for design awareness and object collection.

The City Artist as a Resource. The urban environment houses and supports the majority of visual artists. They may become the resources, the in-house experts for city art programs. For the urban child, the artist as well as his visual statement may become a reality. The accessibility of the artist in the city opens up for inspection his places of work (lofts, studios, places of business, printshops, foundries, and places of exhibits—museums, galleries). Large art supply stores are especially interesting in the city for the art student. The student may not only see the range of possible supplies but also the artist involved in the serious task of material selection. A large number of artists work in nontraditional urban scrap and industrially produced materials. To search for similar materials may lead to the investigation of warehouses, lumber yards, hardware stores, and other places of interest.

The "bigness" of city art may indicate a desire to become involved beyond the decoration of private homes and galleries. The urban artist in his work experiences the desire not only to decorate but to form and shape the foundations of his environment.

The artistic model is not one of a passive observer but an active shaper of the city. It is the importance of the artist to the city that school art may expand. Many urban artists view their work as a means of bringing about significant changes in putting their work into the urban setting.

Art education should not only dwell on self-expression of personal experiences, but also on the communication expressed by the city.

THE VISUAL ORIENTATION OF CITY CHILDREN

The urban child is often a poor reader which may impede his school performance. He possesses, however, a vast storehouse of visual information. Children are extremely sensitive and perceptive to the multitude of visual stimuli of the city. Art education begins with the child's strengths to help him communicate about the things he sees and to form visual statements. The urban child may derive his subject, materials, and inspirations for art experiences from his selections and stimulation of the city.

The School. The child's entrance into the school has many negative effects on visual education. The child in the school is removed from the experiences and stimulation of the environment. During the school day, few direct manipulations or visual experiences are afforded. The environment becomes, to a large degree, a distraction. A classroom is a highly ordered and controlled environment making few concessions to visual needs. Its systems include invisible channels for heat, light, and ventilation providing the necessities for sitting, listening, and reading. Inspirations and observation for the art program are expected to derive chiefly from memory and imagination. This is incongruous with the artistic process which relies on visual stimulations and environmental experiences. As the ties with one's environment and its resources are broken, the quality of art experiences diminishes.

Many of the experiences provided by the school are inappropriate bases for art education. In learning to write, one learns to control the drawn line and restrict it to mechanical patterns of symbol making. Drawing which begins as a form of communication for the child is replaced by writing as the primary means of expression. Manipulative experiences which help the child visually plan and sort his ideas are replaced by written planning. Things become only abstractly connected to the object of thought. Reading, the primary emphasis in elementary education, trains the eye to quickly and systematically decode visual information. It accustoms the child to remove his experience in thinking from what is seen beyond the written symbol. Learning is based on history to information receiving and reviewing of knowledges conveyed by others. The child learns quickly to anticipate what the teacher wants and to follow directions. He is poorly prepared for individual problem-solving responsibilities required for art making.

The expectations of the school are to instruct through quick and well-defined problems and solutions requiring minimal frustration, self-questioning, and involvement. The urban art program is often remedial, putting back the ingredients into the child's experiences which are neglected by schooling. Art programs must consciously reach out into the urban setting for observations and selection for its ideas. It has to involve the city for its artistic models, materials, and processes.

Cars as Urban Objects (charcoal and chalks on paper) 18″ x 24″

The Studio and Home Model. While the city is the inspiration and resource for the artist, he also needs an environment that is less distracting where work can occur. The artist's studio is set up to aid his work. It contains selections of forms and spaces similar to those which will be found in the artwork. The views, the light, and spaces are arranged as the work warrants it.

The complexity of the city places a great deal of importance on the privacy of apartments as important areas to remove oneself to. Apartments become, therefore, a major source of personal expression. People select with care the arrangement and displays of individual objects and collections. Homes involve the continued selection and arrangement of color, texture, form, and light. The apartment is a slice of urban environment under the control of its owner; a control which is often felt lacking over the large urban setting.

Schools often lack the environment that best serves the artwork or the artist, his needs for stimulation, reflection, or movement. Homes and studios can serve as useful models for the school art room. The stimulation and control afforded by both create an ideal place for art making. Both spaces (studio and home) recognize the need for a level of privacy and the need for visual stimulation. Control over one's environment is necessary for one's production. One cannot expect to begin the art process by only giving the child control of his drawing tools. He must be also given freedoms in controlling his environment. The teacher, therefore, must relinquish total control in setting up and arranging the art room to individual artists working within it.

Approaches to Urban Art Teaching. Several strategies may be used in teaching how to investigate aspects of the city. One approach may be to group various aspects of the "inner" urban environment. (The city is comprised of a variety of public and private interiors. These inner spaces such as lobbys, hallways, banks, offices, and railroad terminals are all possible sources for visual investigations.) In the course of a day, children experience a variety of these interiors, all having unique physical qualities, displaying lighting arrangements, decorative styles, etc.

Another approach may be the study of the outside environment. This includes investigation of architectural details of doorways and windows, including their materials and patterns. Observations may focus on various connections from the inner environment to the outer such as doorways, stairs, hallways, canopies, columns, etc. A study may be done of the various orderings of outside spaces including streets, intersections, traffic controls. Changing elements of the outside environment may include its people, traffic lights, and movements.

The study of the city may derive from its most powerful influence—its architecture. In its scale, power, and monumentality, it is the most influential force in the city. The architectural forms, reduced to geometric boxes, may be the symbol and practical basis for elementary school studies. The design of boxes may stimulate architec-

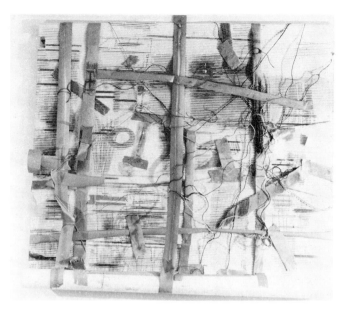

Study of City Streets—A Map (strings, tapes on corrugated roll) 38" x 42"

tural as well as subforms such as packaging, objects of transportation, furniture, etc. While the stacking of boxes represents modern architecture, the inside of boxes represents the homes or interiors we live in. Children may experience the design of personal statements inside the box or more impersonal forms outside of it. A third approach may be the study of art through the collection of urban objects. This may be accomplished by the study of both old and new antiques which derive from the theme of the city.

Working from a Familiar Base. Children are familiar with certain aspects of the city. Their territory, however, is often a limited one and their familiarity cannot be equated with visual awareness. The child often takes his environment for granted, and moves through it routinely, depending on his functional vision. Art education has to make the child's urban experience a visual one.

Ventilation System—Painted Construction Based on City Form (tempera on cardboard) 24" x 24"

The city is often as frightening as it is familiar to the child. In its scale, complexity, and rapid changes over which he appears to have no control, it surpasses his scale and imagination. Art education may help in the formulation of visual understandings to help the child make sense out of the complexity. Artistic studies allow a sense of control in the observation and manipulation of urban forms. Art is valuable in the examination of the many visual systems of the city, e.g., its grids, patterns, modular constructions, and geometry. The continuous environmental changes often leave urban children in a sense of disequilibrium. When the child creativety participates in planning or formulating some of these changes, it becomes less frightening for him.

Contemporary art's most notable feature is the rapid change of styles and movements (which like the city is frightening to its observers). The study how the city affects children in art education, in terms of the acceptance of change, is to lay a foundation for an understanding of contemporary art.

Observing, Recording, and Remaking the Urban Setting. In order for an art program to base itself on the urban setting, children have to become "students of the city." *Observation exercises* may serve as the means of "focusing in," or of conducting detailed studies of the environment. Observations may be made through graphic media including sketches, tracings, and rubbings, or through multimedia approaches including photographs, film, or tape recordings. Observations are to encourage the formation of personal viewpoints. To further stimulate visual discoveries, art problems may stress the selection, sorting, and evaluation of observations recorded. Actual city projects or problems should be used as the basis for planning and redesigning experiences. The development of a range of possible solution ideas based on existing forms and observations may be the basis for art studies. Opportunities for implementation of plans and ideas which may be installed or channeled back into the environment are necessary. For example, plans for a large-scale mural, an outdoor sculpture, or playground equipment may be realized by their being built in the school yard. Collections of objects, materials, photographs, and artworks may be used to broaden one's visual references and provide the opportunity for visual choosing and arrangements.

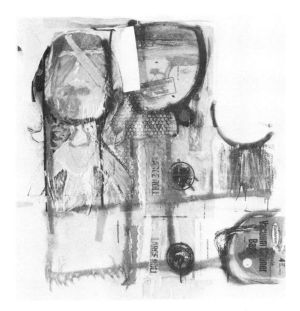

Reflections of Shop Windows (tempera craypas,
plastic bags, cellophane and paper) 24″ x 38″

ART TEACHING AS NONVERBAL COMMUNICATION

All city children should become both verbally and visually literate. The art class may become the training ground for visual emphasis. Akin to lowering the volume controls of a television receiver to emphasize its visual statements, the art teacher may minimize verbal communications in the class in favor of visual channels.

The following four communication channels are available to all art teachers:

Channel One—Materials. Channel One is based on the practice of careful material selection in the planning of a piece. Paintings, for example, begin well before the brush stroke strikes the canvas. Important selections regarding the outcome are made by the painter. Similarly, materials are also selected by the art teacher, choices of which have great determination on the outcome of children's work. Selected materials can elicit certain responses from children, while discouraging others. The painter decides on brushes, paints, and canvases according to texture, size, and shape—each decision forming the work's outcome.

The art teacher's decisions must be equally deliberate; children respond in different ways to materials, depending on their size, shape, familiarity or availability. While the painter arranges his canvas, paints, and brushes with care, e.g., canvas can be shaped, draped, stretched, or rolled according to the perceived outcome, the teacher's planning has to envision similar outcomes in order for materials to communicate successfully.

In Channel One, the art teacher not only selects materials and objects to be used in the art process, but also arranges and displays the selection. Through the arrangement of the materials (codification), the student receives information about the lesson. The selection process both determines and is determined by the objectives of the lesson that is to be taught.

Thus, Channel One is thought of as the materials and objects of the art process. This includes a large array of materials available to the teacher in various sizes, shapes, colors, and textures. Also, communication possibilities exist with reference to combination, placement, juxtaposition, and amount of the materials.

Materials communicate to the student by their very nature: feeling, shape, size, smoothness, hardness, etc. Therefore, the teacher selects materials according to aspects of size, shape, texture, and color. The teacher first selects materials that most clearly express the concept or idea to be communicated. The teacher then determines the most effective placement of the materials chosen. (Materials should be displayed so as to clarify the concept—if there is any possible ambiguity.) Materials should be displayed so as to eliminate the possibility of detracting from the message.

Materials chosen should be considered for their aesthetic appeal. They should invite touch, manipulation, and rearrangement through their colors, shapes, and textures.

The arrangement or placement of the materials should also communicate a style or technique to be used. The combination and sequencing of the materials should imply what is to be done and how it is to be done. (To use a very primitive example—a chalkboard with well-known but incomplete words on it invites completion if chalk is nearby.)

Materials displayed may also be presented altered from their known, original state. This may invite action of the type that will restore the original state. This action may, in turn, lead to creation; i.e., recreation leading to creation.

The teacher is not limited in Channel One to conventional art supplies. A large variety of materials, which may not be traditionally considered as school art supplies, may be used to carry art messages. In fact, the more familiar the object, the greater the chance that the student will know how to use it.

Classroom surfaces can even be among the possibilities of materials used for art communication. Walls, floors, ceilings, and desks suggest processes that can be used in conjunction with other types of materials and objects.

Channel Two—Space. Channel Two involves the *preparation of spaces* and environments for art processes and communication of art processes. Classroom space can direct student attention to art "investigations" in the classroom. They can direct movement to the work, or suggest the amount and types of movements to be performed. Spaces can provoke interest in themselves, or in the activities and materials contained in them. Classroom space is flexible and contains different "visual clues"; thus, the teacher who is interested in creativity should keep the space flexible but well structured with familiar symbols.

In planning the space, the teacher should diagram placement and order of materials, objects, and movements to be used. Space can be structured to reflect movements and steps an art problem involves; space arrangements can define the number of participants; space can be structured to manifest feelings and moods that may underline a solution to a problem; and arrangement of space can define the scale and size of the work.

In planning an expressive space, one is shaping the artwork itself: space can describe or emphasize neighboring spaces; the level of organization in spaces can directly influence the nature and intensity of the product; or space can be shaped and densified to give greater or less visual clarification of the problem. Arrangement of space can also focus any or all of the following: movement, light, and direction. The amount of expressiveness depends, of course, on the message—how it necessitates an expressive environment for its understanding.

The art teacher must be aware of the communicatin factors of a space—such as its size, density, light, and texture. It must be decided what materials and objects are to fill the space (how Channels One and Two are to be combined). It must be decided how a space becomes an environment, how the space is to serve as a communicator of an artist's inspiration, and how the space will motivate individual or group interest in an art problem.

Art room appearances and arrangements present particular atmospheres which communicate by having the student anticipate what he will confront in the room with regard to work and people. If there is a special arrangement, the student anticipates a new goal or process. The student anticipates new functions of even the same materials and objects in the room. (For example, canvases on easels with open jars of paint beside them may signal the student to begin painting; the same scene with closed jars of paint means wait for the teacher to give directions. Easels and canvases stacked near a door may suggest that they are to be moved somewhere.) Thus, function is defined by objects in a space—but more specifically by how they are arranged in a space.

Art-related movements can be arranged through the manipulation of classroom spaces using barriers or other physical arrangements regulating movement. Movement can be constricted or made to flow with greater speed. Rows of work tables, for example, make one aware of a rigid system. It directs attention to a specific way of doing things. An open room, on the other hand, without much furniture, makes the occupants aware of the available space and induces interaction of movement and work.

While a rigid system of rows of work tables presents one set of problems, open arrangements have other problems. An open space incites decoration, a "filling in" of the space, even a transformation of the space. An open space not carefully structured may invite a number of individual choices—generally, a freer, more open solution to art works. The teacher must work harder at channeling and developing aesthetic sensitivity rather than being concerned with activities which are ramifications of other human endeavors.

Channel Three—Teacher Performance. Channel Three refers to communicative acts which can be used to elicit creative responses. It involves the art teacher, now, rather than the materials and objects or the spaces in which the materials and objects are arranged. It involves the art teacher performing creatively. It involves the art teacher directly inspiring creative acts.

In this channel, the art teacher performs along with the students. Materials and objects are still used to elicit action and excite. Spaces are still structured so that action is suggested.

In Channel Three, the teacher plans movements and activities. In a sense, the teacher is choreographed into these movements and interactions are structured. Some interactions may be aleatoric, others more sequentially planned. Students can draw directly on the art teacher's work, or the art teacher can freely draw on the work of students without the student feeling criticized or competitive.

The teacher's movements and actions in the room are used to exemplify the artistic method and illustrate various possibilities with regard to the piece under consideration. The art teacher freely ventures into student "territory" and shares in the solution of art problems. Rather than students being an audience to a performance (as in the case in lecture-demonstration), very often, creative actions are planned which involve both the teacher and the students. Art techniques are acquired by the students, as the teacher and students share in trying to solve art problems.

The child should have a clear perception of the art problem and processes. The problem to be solved should instruct as well as involve the child. The structure should be clear enough so that the teacher's actions do not confuse the student. The objects, materials, spaces, and environments should have enough familiarity so that students know what the teacher is doing and why he is doing it. All this involves careful planning.

Care in planning includes design of a problem that visually includes the teacher and students, in order that the students will feel comfortable in sharing work surfaces, materials, and process. Unlike Channels One and Two, the problems are resolved jointly through the cooperation of the group.

However, the student must not be alienated by a display of complicated materials or dazzled by the teacher as a performer. In the teacher's performance, the processes and techniques should be simple in order for ideas and concepts to be clearly communicable. In other words, enough frustration should be "built-in" or structured so that the students feel a need to call upon the teacher for assistance. The students and teacher are able to share in solving the problem (rather than the teacher merely demonstrating what is to be done).

During the process of the group sharing in a solution, comunication takes place. The teacher communicates feelings, attitudes, and other nonverbal aspects of behavior: (a) smiling, nodding, and patting, (b) spontaneously reacting to something a student has done, (c) carefully examining work, (d) comparing two different solutions to a problem, (e) completing something that is almost, but not quite, finished, and (f) obtaining a sample of a similar solution from a different class.

It would be best in this channel to emphasize nonfigurative rather than realistic representations of subject matter. Demonstrations of artistic ability could deal with arrangements, creative manipulations, visual thinking, and ways of working out problems. In this way, students can immediately respond and share in the activity, rather than being an "audience" to a demonstration. The initial forces set into motion by the structuring of materials, objects, and spaces are now supported by creative actions of the art teacher. With minimal assistance, the students should perceive possible solutions to the art problem.

Channel Four—Evaluation. Channel Four deals with appraisal and evaluation. Students are taught, nonverbally, to compare and judge.

Students are afforded a visual and tactile review of an art problem. This channel is designed to include a series of fact-finding exercises focusing attention on the details, design, media, and technique used in the production of a work. Below are some approaches.

Photographs and Photostats. Photographs and photostats permit reworkings of a problem. Reproduction helps the eye focus sequentially on the process, seeing details not readily available at a glance. In addition, the teacher and students can trace and draw over a photostat or xerox copy.

The evaluation process encourages reproduction mechanically through photostats, reproductions, film, slides, photographs, and tracings. Reproduction leads to the understanding of complex elements and their relationships that compete for attention. In reproducing or approximating, details are simulated. If the students are involved in this reproduction, it is even better. The physical involvement provides interest and the time necessary for art evaluation. Tracings may be used to collect visual data from the artwork or its reproductions. With each tracing, there is a residual product such as a collection of shapes, lines, or colors. Seeing the elements removed from the original work allows for visual comparisons.

In Channel Four, as in previous channels, it is recommended that the group process be used in examining the product. Many more nonverbal communications are possible in the group process. Nods of approval are frequent; eyes light up, children make exclamations, children shake each other's hands as visual discoveries are exchanged.

Estimating. In the reevaluation process, the artist may make visual "estimates" and comparisons. The students may test their estimates by tearing or cutting facsimilies and placing them on the original work. Colors and lines may similarly be examined by matching strings, wires, and paint swatches alongside similar qualities in an artwork.

A Puzzle Approach. Reproductions may be cut or torn apart and the pieces reassembled. This process encourages consideration of the work's design, how pieces fit into a total scheme that makes up an individual artwork. The disassembling may be guided by a number of qualities displayed in the work; the major divisions of color, light, or spaces.

Coloring Book Approach. Coloring "over" a projection or reproduction of the artwork clarifies understandings that may be disregarded visually. This process may cover subject and details but clarify major movements and reveal structure. In attempting to rediagram an artwork, one is not only remaking the surface of the work, but develops an understanding of the underlying work and its maker. In attempting to duplicate the artist's steps, one reverses the art process of continuous elaboration of an idea. The result is a sense of a "peeling away" layers of the artist's experience and understandings. In the coloring process, close attention must be paid to selecting materials and processes that approximate the original works.

Artworks under evaluation may serve to stimulate individual judgments and appreciations. Students, at this time, have the opportunity to record their perceptions and reactions through several means.

Visual Note-Taking. Art appreciation performed nonverbally needs a means of eliciting reactions to the work which may be "voiced" visually. This process in evaluation moves away from the work, steps back from direct manipulations to recording, diagramming, or sketching. The drawings visually clarify as well as represent individual reactions. Through the sharing of individual responses between the teacher and student, personal judgments are formulated. Visual notes attempt to make evaluative thinking visible, reminding the participants that a great deal of decision making in the arts is a visual phenomenon.

The art products need not necessarily be hung or shown by the teacher. The teacher can structure the room so that the students will know they are to select the best works. For example, picture hooks may be installed in a row with paintings available in a corner. The teacher may hang one and employ the necessary body language to encourage other choices for display.

The artist's involvement in work-related evaluations is not primarily to pass judgment but is a learning experience directed at improving his own production. A third type of evaluation concerns itself with the application of evaluative learnings to new artworks.

The Application Process. The findings of visual investigations from previous artworks may serve as a direct basis for new art productions. Another approach may be the used photographs of previous artworks to inspire new production. The photographs may serve as records of what has already been done as well as providing a means of comparisons.

The difference in size between a photograph and the original artwork adds a different dimension to the goal of Channel Four—affording a visual and tactile review of an art problem. First, students manipulate a representation of the original artwork and there is a different tactile sensation. Secondly, students perceive the details in a different perspective. Thirdly, students have to fit the artworks into a new "gestalt" creating additional problems and possibilities.

As previously stated, xerox copies of the artworks can be made, and using these copies, students can make further corrections and elaborations. In order to set forth new ideas, the students are forced to reexamine past compositions. With each new step, there is a retracing and rediagramming of the original work's direction.

Evaluation and sorting of opinions have traditionally been the most verbal and language-oriented procedures in art teaching. In this system, the model used is not the critic of art but the artist himself, thus making visual considerations using art processes possible. When the artist is used as a model, there occurs a union between the making of art and the appreciating or criticism of it.

The project approach not only facilitates evaluation but is an important aid to socialization and an escape from isolation.

Comparisons. In helping the student develop personal taste, he is exposed to the art responses of the artist-teacher as well as other participants. He is encouraged to make selections and become aware of the selections of others.

Works can be hung, exhibited, or collected in portfolios allowing for sortings and comparisons. Comparisons can be structured between the children's own works, between the work of the children and the teacher, or between the work of the teacher and other adult artists.

A Gallery Approach. In critical examination of the work, the artist may visually diagram or extract from the work's structure information he may further employ in art production. The student needs similar opportunities of selection.

As a cue or signal that appraisal and evaluation are taking place, paintings, slides, film, or photographs may be displayed as in a museum or gallery. The environment is carefully planned so students know that finished or almost finished works are being displayed.

THE BILINGUAL ART PROGRAM

New York City and other urban centers conduct school programs in a variety of languages. The bilingual program is an attempt to insure that the non-English speaking child will have a continuity in his education and that the pride and traditions of individual cultures will be maintained.

Entrance to school and society is often viewed as a verbal phenomena. The comprehension and relationship to one's new visual environment is seldom considered. The visual shock of entering into a city may be equally severe as the loss of verbal language. Bilingual programs emphasize a two-language approach to reading and language arts. This approach dwells on the child's weakness instead of his strengths.

Children inherit the visual aspect of American culture very quickly. The *conversion* is made possible most successfully by the environment, and is speeded by the various media. The child learns, therefore, to read "the American-scene way" before he can converse. The new visual world which the child becomes interested in and excited about becomes the starting point for art communications.

Art forms have unique abilities that allow them to be excellent "communicators." In their manipulative states, they are capable of storing various traces of communication. In their arranged states, they are capable of summarizing "communications." The information recorded in art media may be taped or turned to by perceptive others. Art forms traditionally considered as personal states are capable of embodying responses as well.

The attempts to maintain the child's heritage are often defined in terms of language. Bilingual children have an equally important visual and artistic heritage which may form the base and content of the art program.

The Art Teacher in a Bilingual Program. Art teachers in bilingual schools are asked to learn second and third languages in an attempt to continue a verbal style art teaching. As language communication is disrupted, the art teacher has a valuable opportunity to communicate his subject visually. When lessons are planned for visual comprehension, the art teacher is forced to consider the visual content of the subject.

Art is a universal language, a means of communication which the art teacher may apply to a bilingual setting.

While the art teacher may master the required verbal languages, it will seldom be learned in such depth as to converse in the technological language of art. Through visual performances, the teacher not only communicates an art lesson but is able to demonstrate himself as the artist in the class.

The Non-English Speaking Child and Art Education. The non-English speaking child feels abandoned in a classroom without a means of communication. These children are often shy and embarrassed about what they feel is a disability. They often avoid the teacher's direct glances and the attempts to fire language at them which they do not comprehend. Facial expressions speak of embarrassment and inadequacy.

For many teachers, the ability to speak the English language is crucial. The inability is often looked upon as a sign of not being intelligent. In the face of the child's bewilderment with language, the teacher continues with frustrating monologues, often alienating the child completely. Our entire body is a "communicator" as well as a receiver of information. As communication is disrupted it acts as a line of defense which often visibly signals the scars of frustration in its inability to complete communication functions. The non-English child becomes suspicious, angry, and disappointed with himself and others when he is not able to partake in conversations.

On the other hand, art is communicated through the extensions of our body into materials and spaces. Therefore, there is a removal of the pressures of direct communication; the embarrassment of a face-to-face conversation. It removes exchanges from the child's already vulnerable body. Art communications not only allow communications on a universal level (all children are able to draw), but more importantly, they do not appear to deal directly with the child but with his work, his product, or extensions of himself. Art communications further reduce communication pressure by making exchanges into shared experiences instead of a direct volley of words. With a far more relaxed form of communication, conversation becomes less self-conscious and far more revealing. The familiarity with art for the child does not appear to have the same connotations generally associated with language, such as written exams. Art is always considered to be "fun," where the non-English speaking child does not feel judged or examined in any way. Art communications, in their openness, manage to reveal not only the child as seen by the teacher, but the art teacher as seen by the child.

Art conversations disregard accents, differences in vocabularies, or patterns of speech that tend to differentiate people in this society even after some language has been learned.

Drawing as Communication—Work by Student and Teacher (watercolor and chalk on paper) 18″ x 25″

A CONTEMPORARY ART BASE FOR ELEMENTARY TEACHERS

Art Education should concern itself with the art world of today and with the possibility of forming a bridge with the art world of the future. If the child's art education is to be relevant to the contemporary visual world, the school has to train for an understanding of the artist today. Contemporary art concepts should form the basis of learning strategies.

The work of contemporary artists holds a significant place in society. However, it often has little input into the school art program. School art is often based on projects and problems conceived of in school but having little relationship to the art world outside. "School art" can be characterized by "macaroni pictures," anything pasted down called a "collage," and a large array of works called "Abstracts." While the contemporary artist is increasingly more dependent on a highly perceptive and educated public, art teachers in the schools express little empathy for the contemporary art world. The filtering down of *visual research* by contemporary artists to the schools is an extremely slow process. At the same time, the art world is changing at an unprecedented rate forming an increasingly wider gap between the training in the schools and the reality of the art world.

Schools prefer to deal with certainties with proven approaches, and are seldom forces of change. In the case of art education, if schools continue to teach what has come to be accepted by the masses in society, then a whole generation of potential art audiences will be lost. Children visiting a gallery or museum, looking at contemporary architecture or fashion design, will feel no connection between their school experience and the teachings of the artist. Art education must deal with the abstract uncertainties of the art world, because uncertainty is what contemporary art is all about. School art sometimes stays away from the abstract, in its concern for clarity (using verbal standards as a measure for school works).

Art should not follow the verbal logic of the school. Its principles cannot always be clearly and rationally defined in verbal terms. Art that cannot be broken down into formulas and quick comprehension meets with dubious approval. Since contemporary art is such a vast area of study, it cannot be relegated to a single "appreciation" course, and is usually postponed until secondary education. To wait until the child reaches an adult stage is too late, because opinions about most of the visual environment have already been formed.

Contemporary Concerns of Artists. The subject of contemporary artworks is familiar to children since they are based on contemporary forms and media themes. Even in the most abstract works, the city is revealed in its scales, forms, colors, and materials. The contemporary artist, through large-scale simple forms, invites the viewer to partake in the timeless concerns of artists. Through their works, contemporary artists educate their public with regard to the basic values of art (structuring with lights, shapes, colors, textures, and lines)—which are appropriate lesson materials for elementary art teaching, since it is in the elementary school that the child's enjoyment of form, color, and line begins to diminish. By de-emphasizing the subject and returning to simple minimal forms, the artist allows his work and the attention of the audience to return to the true concerns of art. For example, in elementary school art, a return to the basics can mean an extension of the child's play with materials; finger painting may be brought to an advanced level by encouraging more sophisticated play with materials (i.e.,

Stained Painting (acrylics, food color on soft paper and cloth)
18" x 36"

to explore new ways of applying paint without applying a brush to a canvas); the game of block-playing may be extended with the introduction of more sophisticated design concepts.

Another approach derived from contemporary art is to work with available objects or forms, thus making the problem of a subject less important. This may mean beginning with a "given" situation and using it to start the art problem.

An elementary school child yields to the school's verbal demands and uses art in a story-telling manner. He is continuously called upon to explain his artwork; "what is it?", "what are you making?", "what does it look like?", "how do you explain your work?" Questions calling for responses demand a verbal subject matter explanation. In school, artwork that is not comprehensible to others in terms of a story or theme is seldom valued as art. Henceforth, the principle enjoyment and reward for the child's efforts is not in his design of form or statement of color, but in his ability to use form and color to represent something else.

Contemporary art also yields the possibility of *directing a child's effort back into his original concern with materials, processes, and design.* The child can be challenged to arrive at a work of a certain scale or to discover new methods of layering colors. Such a change of expectation can change the child's own emphasis. In working with ready-made objects, a child may be taught to reproduce subjects through simple mechanical means such as photography, light boxes, tracings, rubbings, or projections; he thus quickly involves himself in design with art elements. Three-dimensional ready-made objects may be wrapped or covered, so that the form covering will be discovered and the child's attention will again freely move to a design emphasis.

Three Chairs—Reflections on Form (tempera on chair wrapped in paper)

Having clearly defined an actual subject allows one to probe further. And this is exactly what some contemporary artists (pop, minimal, etc.) have done with their audiences. Such artists, in essence, have freed color, form, and light from subject limitations, instructing their viewers to go beyond the minimal subject concern.

Free Expression in Conceptual Art. The abstract expressionist movement of the 1940s and '50s had a profound influence on school arts. Its approaches and often misinterpreted doctrines are still the major force in the elementary school art class. Abstract expressionism is interpreted as self-expression and the encouragement of free and spontaneous use of materials. Self-expression is often equated with creativity in its appeal to the subconscious and intuitive manner of works. In the name of self-expression, all works by children were accepted and were beyond comment or criticism. Approaching artwork in an intuitive manner is, in itself, an important creative choice. The abstract expressionists planned for their freedom and accidental effects. The experience of painting in this style has important decision points requiring planning and self-criticism. It required the addition of elements to a canvas or sculpture but equally the removal or opening up of new possibilities. School art, in treating the whole process as a series of accidents, often asks children to combine all types of materials in layers of paint which becomes frustrating and often impossible to meaningfully resolve. The impression children receive from art is often that it is thoughtless, messy, and illogical. While gaining a degree of freedom in work habits, they are not fully exposed to the art process.

Contemporary art rejects the abstract expressionist concern for the free brush stroke, the accidental effect and the combined preoccupation with the free display of one's emotions. It is instead highly rational and conceptual in its approach and style. The artists of op, minimal, and conceptual art emphasize the idea being as important as the action or the process. Contemporary art has a machine-made, mass-produced appearance revealing little of the artist's hand, demonstrating little of his experiment. Styles are expressions of their makers, yet contemporary expressionism appears through a ruler and T-square to express formal arrangements and rational personal choices. Some children prefer this more conceptual and less messy way of working.

Artistic expression is, to various degrees, a combination of the free and intuitive as well as the conceptual and controlled.

Children should be exposed to the entire contemporary range of art ideas and left to decide their preferences. Contemporary conceptual approaches have the advantage of having children recognize that the artist deals with emotions as well as with visual ideas.

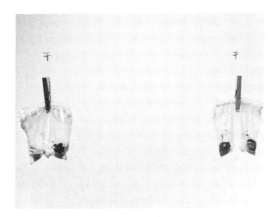

Play Experiments with Paint (tempera and sand in sealed plastic bags) 2″ x 4″

The New Subject and the School. Contemporary art's response to the city has expanded the lists of subjects considered appropriate for art to include almost everything. One approach has been to appropriate the most banal objects and enlarge them in scale. These objects include detergent boxes, beer cans, and comic book characters. Many contemporary subjects appeal to children raised by the media. The changes of these objects when placed into an art context include manipulations of scale, changes in color, simplification, and repetition. The subjects are mechanically reproduced, many of the techniques appropriate to elementary art problems. More abstract subjects are geometrical forms or boxlike shapes and the stripe surfaces of architectural forms found in the city. This subject may be directly explored by children through references to their own geometric-linear environment.

The use of objects in contemporary art works has several special features. Objects are treated as a whole and expressed life size or larger. The emphasis is on its objectness, sometimes emphasized by shaping the canvas into the form of the object or using glossy mechanically applied surfaces. Some artists used the actual object itself, therefore calling attention to the process of selection as an art form. Although the use of objects has been frequent in school art in the form of collages, the collage treatment has not dealt with the object itself but the colors and textures collected as it was cut into pieces.

The contemporary artists give everyday "city forms" new dignity. In their simplicity, they allow an in-depth exploration beyond their casual meaning. Most of the new subject matter emphasizes newness (shininess) of the mass-produced objects, in essence challenging the elementary art program's frequent use of garbage as its raw material.

Elementary Art as a Preparation for the Understanding of Contemporary Art. The messages of contemporary artists can only be received by an educated audience. Contemporary art education is relegated to the secondary school or college art appreciation courses. Adults who have lost significant contact with the arts often find it difficult to be visually receptive to the contemporary artist. It is the elementary school child who would best profit from the experiences and exposures of artists since in many respects they are closer to them.

Material and process experiments performed in elementary school develop a valuable readiness stage for current art ideas. This foundation is important because of the rapid change in styles the elementary child of today will be exposed to in the future. Art training, for children, has to develop open minds and take the time and effort in forming responses and opinions to artworks. They must learn not to be frightened and close out what is not easily and immediately understood.

Art education should also stress the general development of the senses. Visual messages are only received by those who have developed a sense of visual awareness. Artworks can only be made by those who have a developed sense of tactile, sound, and smell awareness.

Readiness for contemporary art also means training for environmental awareness. This includes being able to use the environment as a resource for art ideas, to be able to decode prominent features of form, color, etc., and to see relationships to each other and contemporary art. Space awareness is to consider shapes, feel, and color of various spaces and its effects on the user. The process of selection and collection of materials and objects should be emphasized as an art in itself. Experimentation should be recognized as an art process regardless of its final outcomes.

Painting Explored as a Three-Dimensional Object
(watercolor on shaped cardboard) 24″ x 40″

The Interrelationship of the Arts. Visual artists may no longer be clearly identified as painters, sculptors, or craftsmen. Paintings have become three-dimensional, sculpture has gained color and an architectural appearance. Painters use commercial methods of working, architects are making sculpture using methods and specifications of the industrial designer. Art programs in the school have to adopt an integrated curriculum in the arts. This should include investigations as to similarities in aims, techniques, tools, and other commonalities of the artists. This type of approach is to introduce the principle that multiple ways may be used to express all art ideas. The techniques and materials selected for any particular problem should be freely governed by the art idea. To hope to understand the art of the future, a broad view across all the arts is necessary since ideas and innovations may come from the fashion artist, the painter or the architect and be quickly adopted by other artists. Examples in relating an art problem should always be drawn from a variety of visual artists.

Issues in Contemporary Art. Major issues in contemporary art which may be appropriate for elementary school investigations both in its theory and practical experiences may include: serialization (systems approach), simplification, and symmetrical arrangements; students may also investigate geometrical or minimal forms, shaped canvases, and color-field paintings.

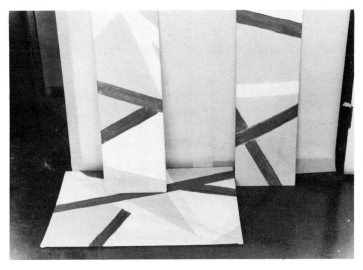

Rectangles Divided by Stripes (tempera, masking tape on paper covered syrofoam) 14″ x 36″

CHAPTER FIVE

Play as a Model for Art Teaching

Concept: The child learns best in a play situation. The art class may stimulate many of the instincts and qualities displayed in play, notably the spontaneity of the heart and mind, the self-directiveness which allows one to set one's own problems and follow through to conclusion. The art room can be the place where play may continue after the child enters the serious work of schooling. The art room may remain open to foster the kinds of ideas and situations in which the child learns best.

PLAY AS A NATURAL FORM OF EXPRESSION

Through positive play experiences, the child develops all the necessary traits to prepare him for creative tasks. The child who fears failure in art probably has come from poor play experiences. During the early play stages of the child's life, he is the most creative and least inhibited in his play. The rest of the child's creative life may be seen as an attempt to recapture or keep alive this period. In this respect at one time we were all artists or creative people. Play more specifically develops the qualities of:

challenge	anticipation	competition	goal
stimulus	observation	motivation	promise
timing	improvisation	curiosity	interest
excitement	abstraction	coordination	skill
reward	exploration	discretion	analysis
perception	concentration	discrimination	judgment
restraint	fulfillment	enjoyment	patience

The Retardation in School of Art, Play, and Creativity. The school views itself as a place to introduce and indoctrinate the child into the world of work. It also trains the child to be proficient in school so as to prepare for more schoolwork. Children entering school are expected to be serious and dedicated and to discard all that is fun or interesting. Instead, the school offers "learning and knowledge" derived from others as transmitted by the teacher. Play, in school, is branded as frivolous. What is taught is what is measurable and clearly definable.

The school emphasizes mastery, authority, and control, while play is concerned with freedom and self-direction. These two courses appear clearly incompatible. Neither play nor art comes prepared with ready answers, quick explanations, or the clarity characteristic of most school endeavors. When the emphasis in school turns to prescribed understandings, play quickly ceases. When play is not practiced or encouraged, it disappears; and with it often the creative spirit dies.

When one's own original solutions and ideas are seldom exercised or given equal consideration to "ready-made learnings," one quickly forgets one's own capabilities to create original and unique solutions. In the process of being "educated," we forget how to freely explore and experiment—qualities both essential to art making. The school makes the child a passive listener, a quiet note taker and not an active player or thinker. Spontaneous curiosity is often replaced by readily available problems and solutions. *The art class must be structured so that play can continue.*

Recapturing the Joy and Dedication to Play. The art class must be dedicated to keep play alive by its reward and attention given to it. Since the child entering school is neither encouraged nor rewarded for play, he begins to develop an important distinction between play and work, between what he likes to do and what has to be done. It must be recognized that all great inventions and ideas in the visual arts require the elements of play to bring them about. The child must know that his playful instincts are valued in the art class. The art class may be considered as "remedial" play for children whose play has been seriously disrupted by school. Through the use of the art room space, its materials and processes, play can be reintroduced.

The popularity of art classes has long been based on the joy it brings to students. In play tasks, the child simply enjoys what he is doing and consequently brings to his art a sense of dedication. These rewards cannot be compared in significance to the artificial rewards brought about by "extra credits" or a grading system. Children in the art class may begin to realize that there is nothing childish about play which is very much the activity of a creative adult.

DEVELOPMENT OF PLAY SKILLS

The development of one's play skills may be approached on several levels: (1) maintaining a positive attitude and value towards play activity, (2) providing the opportunity for play including the design of art teaching where children learn to set their own problems and follow them through, and (3) introducing play problems designed to exercise the play instinct designed by the teacher.

Sharpening Play Skills. Play skills can be sharpened by directing art learning into: (a) self-directed or free play, where the child is able to select materials, work space, and technique; (b) directed play where some basic rules or guidelines provide the discipline and part of the motivation; and (c) group play, where the communication between players (student to student, teacher to student) may be through the media of art resulting in the evolvement of new art forms.

Nourishment and Exercise for Play. Play utilizes visual forms as its media for exploration. The child needs a wide variety of interesting materials to conduct his investigations. He also needs a variety of interesting spaces including an open conception of time and a sense of privacy. Play may be designed to involve all the senses including provisions for touch, smell, sight, and sound. Play exercises may use art media to test reality, explore and expand it, study the nature of forms, colors, textures, and spaces.

A great deal of play experimentation is time consuming and to an outsider apparently fruitless. The efforts may not be measurable in the resulting product. Patience, time, and acceptance nourish discoveries. Great ideas have to be "played out" because they are not known in advance. An important aspect of play is to keep open the trial-and-error phase in art and teaching children not to be content or settled with quick and easy solutions. A great deal of satisfaction has to come from the play itself without expectation of results or pushing for finished products. Sharing the play experience with others through verbal, photographic, or drawing means may be a good basis for the child's reviewing of his play session.

Play for Problem Solving. Specific problems in play often challenge the player to generate a range of solution ideas. Interesting materials, a demand for an unusual size or scale or a reference to an imaginative subject may all

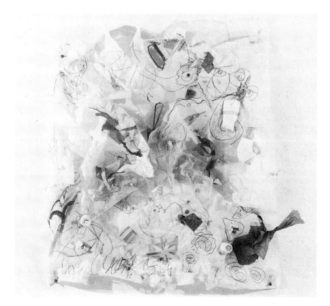

Play with "Crumpled" Layers of Tracing Paper (cray-pas and objects mounted on tracing paper) 34" x 34"

initiate the problem. Limitations may be in terms of size, shape, color, material, etc. Ground rules for play may be set in advance, requiring perhaps several versions and selections of the desired outcome. Play should not be hampered by strict requirements of craft or finished quality. Materials for play may limit the use of adhesives or permanently bonding materials until some later point so that forms may be taken apart, reassembled many times before being permanently fixed. The art teacher must value the possible solutions or the ideas that have been generated, giving them the same attention as the finished product.

Play to Share Personal Experiences. Through playing with art materials, one gains access to inner thoughts and feelings. Play can be designed to share these experiences with other players or audience. Feedback from others helps to broaden the scope of one's play and gain greater insight into one's work. Through the manipulation of forms and objects one gains insight into oneself.

Play may be conducted around themes based on personal experiences leading into art experiences that elaborate on these experiences. The display of one's discoveries in play in a more permanent art media may give the player a sense of importance and legitimacy to the play experience. Play may thus be considered a preliminary set of experiences or expressions on its way to becoming art. Play may help to make the experiences we base art upon more vivid and more sharply defined. It broadens the scope from which to select art experiences.

Play to Interpret Environmental Phenomena. Children's play gives them opportunities to manipulate elements of the environment and to make changes in it. Play is a means of reflecting upon the environment and gaining a sense of power over its mastery.

Play creates an environment in miniature. It allows for the scaling down of the real world into a manageable format. Play may be imitative of the environment as well as taking its clues from it. Its discoveries may be compared with the environment itself. The art room set up for play must consider flexibility in its furnishing, partitions, and contents. Children should be able to develop findings of their play in the room's environment. An example follows.

PLAY AND THE FORMATION OF THE ARTISTIC PERSONALITY

The difficult task of creating demands certain personality factors such as self-esteem and self-confidence.

Before one can set and direct one's own creative problems, in building the play factor into art, one becomes accustomed to searching for new discoveries and to accept unknown and untried solutions. Play provides for the necessary pride and self-accomplishment in art. Through playful experimentation with materials, the child is able to freely "mess" and make mistakes. This is a necessary trait for art workings where mistakes require changes, a sense of struggle as the expected nature of the art process. The child also learns that openness and spontaneity in play pay off and may be rewarding in art experiences. Through play, the child also learns concentration and patience necessary in working with forms and ideas which may not be completely clear or understood from the start. Artistic "seeing" and appreciations require the above qualities as well. Through successful play experiences, the child learns to challenge himself in his art media and finds interest and curiosity in the challenge. While manipulating and structuring his play, the child gets used to looking and observing before making subsequent choices.

Failure in Play. The child who has not had positive play experiences will find most self-initiated activities in art threatening. Play provides the necessary groundwork for the child to find enjoyment and satisfaction in creative discoveries. Children who have not had the positive experiences will not explore their artwork fully, tending to give up on themselves quickly and give up on the artwork. Without having the experience of making meaningful choices for oneself through play and expressing these preferences in concrete object form, the child will be uncomfortable with art workings and even basic artistic tasks.

Opportunities in Play for Decision Making. For art to go beyond the stage of intuition, one has to accustom the child to continuous balance between playful selection and firm decision. When play is incorporated into every step of the artistic process, it allows for a continuous stream of possible ideas. These possibilities deal with the essence of art which is to make decisions about visual choices. Every step in the art process can be designed to include aspects of play which will provide an in-depth experience recorded in the artwork.

EXPERIMENTAL FEATURES OF PLAY

The child must be encouraged to stop inquiring or guessing what the teacher wants or has in mind and begin to trust and express his own ideas with confidence. Having the equipment and the necessary tools, the child may develop his own experiments. The teacher may help by expanding play ideas through additional materials, spaces, and verbal suggestions. Play may be furthered by suggestions of new movements (physical) which are ultimately recorded in the work. The teacher may offer general directions to play but an increasing amount of initiative must come from the child continuously instilling the knowledge and responsibility that he is to set his own problems.

To monitor experimentations in play, the teacher may increase or decrease the selection of materials, set limitations on size, scale, color, or complexity of work. Limitations may be arrived at through the introduction of the work of other players or artists. Play experiments may be useful in the development of (a) sensory awareness, (b) organizational skills, (c) observational skills, (d) ability to make visual judgments or choices, (e) generating new inventions, (f) formulating career ideas, and (g) developing environmental awareness.

Play with Cutout Forms (charcoal and painted shapes on paper)
24″ x 36″

Play for Sensory Awareness. A great deal of schooling has the effect of removing the child from primary artistic concerns. The objective of sensory play is the return of the child's attention to artistic concerns with materials, material qualities, colors, textures, and forms. For example, in the study of penmanship, the child moves from his free scribbling line and pleasures of contact with surfaces to a mechanical rendering of his drawing as well as his alphabet. The child who used to listen and feel his materials while drawing becomes merely concerned with the symbols and clarity of his writing. This trend towards legibility in writing expresses the problems in children's play and in artwork where the need for clarity of the idea begins to surpass artistic concerns for line, color, etc. The need for sensory play is remedial to the art program in having the child rededicate his interests in art qualities. Play of this nature should center around materials and their use and not subject content. The teacher's proposals for play may reflect this interest by outlining the use of interesting contrasts or similarities in materials, exploring different physical states of materials and sensory qualities of materials. While the young child in his scribbling stage does not need finger paintings and experiences in the sandbox (both of which he has expertise), the school age child requires these play experiences which have been removed and replaced by school experiences.

Playing to Develop Organizational Skills. The development of organizational skills is to include the construction of three-dimensional forms. These forms can be constructed from plasterboard, styrofoam, lumber, brick, and other building materials. Organizational play may be conducted through materials of similar properties (same colors, shapes) or of different qualities. In planning for arrangements, allowances should be made for expansion in scale, sizes, and directions. Play may take place within defined boundaries such as on a marked floor surface, on a colored base, or inside the box. Games of organization develop compositional ideas of balance, proportion, symmetry, etc.

The construction of elaborate models may be constructed from modular units, geometric, or free forms. Although the sequence of activities may vary, permanent attachment of pieces or the development of a finished product should be de-emphasized. Play periods may conclude by taking photographs, sketches, or rubbings of completed forms which are still left open for modification.

Play to Develop Observational Skills. The artist looks into the environment storing visual information and selects for his work from information he has stored. Art which is expected to magically derive from imagination in

Variations on a Symbol—A Stencil Painting (finger paints and Gesso on paper) 28″ x 32″

fact comes from observations and experiences. The artist is as original as he is a skilled observer. The artist at work relies on a direct setup of still life, models, and other sources of observation. In his involvement with his subject, the artist selects the details which he formally recombines and restructures in his work. Play aids the child in maintaining direct experiences with his subject allowing for observations which may be translated into the artwork. Observational skills develop from the active involvement of play, focusing the child's attention and activity to first-hand visual experiencing. To develop observational skills, the child's play must come in direct contact with the forms and materials to be examined. Wrapping games, for example, allow the child to wrap up forms such as chairs, telephones, and other familiar objects. Seeing the objects in their new forms removes the child from subject connotations. The wrapping allows the viewing of an object from all angles and allows for its understanding as a form.

Play for Environmental Awareness. Play is one of the early means through which the child tests reality. Through play, the child explores his environment by making tentative drawings or models of it. Play is one of the few available means for the child to make choices and actively react to his environment. From birth, the child's surrounding is arranged by parents, teachers, and community. Television describes additional visual settings both real and imaginary for his considerations. The child quickly feels that in passing through life, few environmental

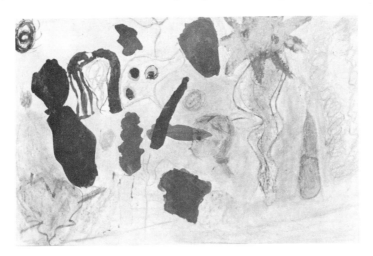

Play with Shapes and Lines—Painting of Still Life Set Up by Child (tempera and chalk on paper) 24″ x 36″

choices are available to him. The development of taste and individual judgment relies to a great extent on having the opportunity to choose.

Play, relating to the environment, may continuously afford the child the opportunity to observe, plan, and implement ideas concerning his environment. One type of play may be the construction of models of homes, classes, streets, and neighborhoods. These models of spaces may become a permanent classroom fixture which may be explored continuously. Indoor models may consider interior spaces including the design and arrangements of furnishings. Outdoor models may plan buildings, develop city plans, and design for urban objects such as signs, shop windows, and street lighting. The art room may afford an opportunity for children to arrange full-scale space designs.

Environmental objects may be collected. Their selection and sorting may be developed into art projects which encourage children to utilize their choices.

Play as an Active Response to Media. Children are passive respondents to media communication. They spend a countless number of hours reviewing television which affords them few opportunities for creative or manipulative response. Many of their play objects are media-oriented; that is, they are designed to perform for them. Children's play may serve as a concrete means to reverse the trend of one-way media flow into a two-way response. Interest in media is high, and therefore it may become a valuable resource for media-related play (working from television images, designing action drawings from the screen).

CONCEPT FORMATION THROUGH PLAY

The abstract expressionist movement in art has emphasized free and expressive qualities as the principle concern of the artist. Intuitive self-expressive approaches became synonomous with art in the schools. Creative expressions through play or art are, in fact, a form of thinking. The ability to combine visual forms requires concept formation. Play begins with an idea or invention and formulates its objectives into forms of aesthetic quality. Through play, the idea in a creative endeavor may gain equal import to decorative qualities. The problem-solving actions result in creative forms.

Play, in school art, may take place through well-defined problems, boundaries, or game plans. Creative limitations challenge the child's play in his attempt to expand them.

The Student as a Recipient of Knowledge vs. the Generator of Original Thought. Education concerns itself with imparting basic skills and subject matter knowledge. Success of it depends on the child's ability to recall and to use ideas removed from his own interest and concern. Through play in the art class, the child may continue to research his own interests and demonstrate his own ideas.

Play for Career Awareness. Often, it has been assumed that the basis for art careers is an exposure to the fine

Play with Lines and Torn Shapes (craypas, chalks on paper roll)
28" x 32"

arts. Based on a survey of the visual environment, children begin to realize that there are many other artists involved in the making of the total visual setting.

Career education should begin in the elementary school with career awareness based on creative play. Play materials may be selected with the various art professions in mind.

The Practice of New Behaviors in Developing New Forms. Through play, the child has available constructive means to practice all types of behaviors. Many behaviors which may be felt to be unacceptable or difficult to express may be channeled through play. New forms are born out of one's ability to freely test one's visions and openly manipulate media. The artist as well as the scientist formalize their behaviors into well-defined experiments. New artistic forms appear as a result of testing new behaviors. Play allows a natural and relaxed climate in which free expression may be practiced.

Play as a Response to Positive Relationships. A sound relationship must be developed between teacher and child as the basis for play activity. The school child quickly learns his role as a worker and becomes reluctant to play. It is not unusual for even young children to exclaim that play is childish. The teacher is not to be an authority or director of play, but another artist who is willing to share in the struggle as well as the findings. The teacher may find interest in the child's discoveries, and champion it in the face of oppositions. The art teacher may be a resource person who may extend materials, space, and idea possibilities. Based on a well-formulated relationship, the child will continuously search for original ideas and will be free to display them. The "child-as-the-artist" needs his or her communications to be well received by the teacher serving as a sympathetic audience. The teacher's role, in encouraging play, means to reestablish confidence in the child's own abilities and to give credence to individual "visions."

PLAY IDEA FILE

Sensory Awareness. Play with liquid paints in various shaped containers, soaking paint through layers of materials, rolling out soft materials, connecting rough or course forms, inflating shapes, dipping materials into paint, letting paint run to form drip shapes. Work in dark boxes or darkened rooms assembling "feeling" puzzles, sculptures, or books, constructing an indoor sandbox using shredded foil and rags.

Space Awareness. Designing objects to walk through, crawl through, or to see through. Connecting planes across room corners, building an indoor tent, creating in it clutter, a sense of openness, or space divisions. Connecting floors to walls, walls to ceilings using linear extensions.

Observational Play. Observing and recording events in various perspectives, looking through various size and shape openings. Collecting objects of similar shapes, details, and arranging displays of the above.

Organizational Play. Play with blocks of similar sizes and shapes placing them into grids. Games to assemble and organize prefabricated or ready-made objects, play to arrange layering or the stacking of forms and developing systems of ordering (linear, vertical, horizontal).

Play with Soft Plastics (plastic paint on plastic and paper)
18" x 22"

Career Awareness. Plays to invent machinery or objects, playing to become various visual artists, role-playing art collector, critic, gallery owner. Taking the position of a client and the reverse role of the artist.

Experimental Play. Play with light including light boxes, passing color through perforations, mixing of color gels, creating simple machines and objects with a variety of movements. Plays designed to make the largest form, the simplest form or the most complex form. Creating a paint set of the most unusual colors and finding appropriate names.

CHAPTER SIX

The Artist as a Model

Concept: The artist best exemplifies the workings of the creative process. The study of the artist should become the basis of art learning and art teaching. In this approach, one must view the artist as a person with unique culture, skills, language, attitudes, motivations, and life styles. For art to be a significant addition to school studies, it must demonstrate its uniqueness in the school setting. The school is a forceful agent in imposing its sameness on teachers, subject areas, and teaching methodologies. Art, when squeezed into the school setting (schedules, routines) often becomes a separate entity from art, unrecognizable when viewed from the reality of the art world and the artist. The study of the artist allows the construction of an ideal model against which school realities may be lifted out of their present state. All future art teachers must analyze such an ideal system based on the artist before they settle into routines of the school program. The following chapter is a suggested model. It should be supplemented by involvement in the art world and with visits with the artists.

STUDY OF THE ARTIST

Art teachers must understand the unique characteristics of the artist to maintain a productive art program. Study of the artist must include personal involvement in the art process and in the art world visiting the artists in

The Teacher as the Model (conte crayon on brown paper bag) 18″ x 24″

their studios, lofts, galleries, and workshops. The artist at work is to be viewed on film focusing in on his environment, tools, procedures of work, movements, and actions. The artist is to be heard both in personal interviewing and on tape speaking about himself, about other artists, and about contemporary art.

The study of the artist is to be conducted at a time when the future art teacher embarks on a field experience in the schools and is challenged to formulate his own ideas about art teaching. The student has to evaluate the ways in which the elementary school art program is similar and is different from the essential qualities of artists and the art world, considering what alignments have to be made to conform to the artistic realities.

The Artist. The artist has always been both a learner in society and its teacher. Based on observations and records, the artist has reflected on his society, selected from its essences to create an exemplary model known as art. The artist's work communicates major ideas and innovations of the past as well as providing illuminations of the future. The artist's communication is visual through a visual language which is able to relay a distinct blend of attitudes and emotions with visions and ideas. The artist's work is both a means of personal expression or contact with himself and form of communication to a variety of audiences—public or clients.

The artist is exemplary in his personal beliefs, dedication, and lifelong experimentation, sharpening his own visions and the insights of others. The artist is unique in his independence of action, his ability to research in depth through the use of visual manipulations and in his general problem-solving abilities.

The artist may be studied through his art products or in the process of making these products, in his relation to other artists, or to the art world. Included in his role is that of a collector, a producer, a promoter, a performer, a learner, and a teacher. The study of the artist may include many of the complex behaviors and attitudes distinctive of him.

The study of the artist is essential for the art teacher in order to become an artist-teacher and be able to develop a program accurate to the artistic model. This study is also necessary to allow the treatment of the students in the art class as artists and thus generally raise the level of the program. While teaching art, it is essential for the teacher to consider himself an artist, the students as fellow artists all directly related to other artists outside the school.

Materials and the Artist. The artist selects his material with care and consideration. Materials are selected with the work in mind and become one of the first important steps in the creative process. The material selected aids the artist in envisioning the nature of his experience. In the school, art materials are too often uniform regardless of the project. Material decisions are made by the art teacher. Each choice of size, color, texture, quality, and quantity predetermines a large part of the finished work. (See p. 73.)

The artist spends a great deal of time in exploring new materials intended for creative use. Important skills in handling new materials are gained and ideas as to their possible uses are formulated. School art often skips erratically from material to material without the child having gained the necessary knowledge and skills. There should be a sequence and repetition in the use of material.

The artist limits his use of material to allow for in-depth exploration and reflect a clear visual statement of his findings. School art programs often make available all materials including varieties of scraps creating a great deal of confusion. Very little is learned about the unique nature of each material since each has its own unique qualities and potential uses.

Therefore, the raw materials for art processing have to be selected with purpose with some notion of their possible uses.

The artist bases his material explorations on the understanding and solutions of similar material uses by other artists. Each time a certain material is used, it is backed up by research and knowledge of what other artists have done with that material. The art teacher should, therefore, demonstrate and provide examples of material use by other artists. It should not be assumed that each time the child receives a material that the total experience should be fresh.

The artist has a great love for materials. He often collects and stores materials for possible later use. The buying trip is often a start for new ideas. School art programs should not start completely from the teacher's material collection but include the students in the gathering, collecting, and purchasing of materials.

Contemporary artists often expand the limits of what has been traditionally considered to be appropriate art materials. The school art experience may help the child to identify all material as potential art material. Materials such as lumber, fencing, plastics, and styrofoam are often more familiar than traditional art supplies and more readily available for school use.

The Artist's Place of Work. The artist's work environment is to be the model for school art programs. The artist's selection of his environment is both functional and aesthetic. Artist's work spaces may be selected and arranged with a specific art profession since each visual artist has different work requirements. The school art room, therefore, has to function as a flexible system in studios, lofts, and workshops. The artist's work space requires a combination of privacy and visual involvement. The artist requires space to step back and look at his work from various viewpoints. Space has to be available so that movements and gestures may be freely accorded on material. The types of movement allowed for in the spaces provided greatly affect the work itself.

The artist's environment is in a state of flux, often having about him finished works (the past), unfinished works (the present), and visible sketches or ideas for the future. The school art setting needs to provide the necessary space for all of the above. Having unfinished work in view allows for the artist's thinking to continuously operate and return to the work at another point with new insights.

The artist arranges his space for visual stimulations specifically related to the work in progress. The stimulation may be in the form of models (human and object) and collections (photographs, artworks, reproductions). School art rooms have to provide for visual references to introduce art problems but also as continued resources throughout the work in progress. Visual resources or collections may be gathered by the individual child to aid him in charting his own course of action.

To allow for individual solutions, the child needs also considerable control over his work space. The art teacher has to consider space as a major contributing factor to the artwork produced within it. The artwork is essentially a recording of the environment in which it was made.

The artist is aware of all the surfaces in his environment as possibilities for use in his work. Artist may select to work on walls, on corners, or floors or to be hung from ceilings. The school art room may leave all these possibilities open.

Artistic Attitudes and Their Relationship to School Art. Artists' attitudes and behaviors often provide important clues to the creative process. For the artist, his work is partially an idea as well as an attitude towards art and art making.

The artist expresses strong feelings regarding his work and often views it with almost missionary dedication. Elementary school art must translate the art experiences in terms of the depth of the artist's feelings in order that strong relationships may be formed between the child and art. The artist in his role as a teacher disperses his teaching through art workings. Each work illuminates to the viewer a statement about the art process, about the artist himself, and his view of the society. For him, his work is a continuous and full-time process. Art, in the school, has to have similar continuity since art learnings are not based on a single art lesson or experience. Art learnings demand a continuous involvement in visual learnings and experiences. In order for art education to be meaningful for the child, it has to become part of his total school experience. This approach demands working on art problems at home as well as in school.

The artist must accomplish a great deal of his work alone. He must formulate ideas, collect object and material resources, record relevant observations, and through a series of independent thoughts and actions work out a visual statement. School art training has to develop this attitude and responsibility to carry out independent work from the start. The student may be accustomed in elementary school to set his own problems and carry them out without overly relying on teachers' rewards and criticisms. Throughout the art experience, the student has to be given a great deal of responsibility in his investigations. Problems should not be posed in a series of steps to a solution, putting forth the notion that the teacher knows the correct procedure or answer and all it takes is simple mastery. Art problems have to be so constructed that each student is able to restate and question for himself each set of directions. Accordingly, rewards must come not for repetition of posed art problems, but for the finding of individual interpretations, the degree of in-depth involvement, and individual solutions.

The artist recognizes his process as one which is full of uncertainties through which he is willing to trust his ideas and intuitions. During the art process, he is willing to take detours, risks, and explore all the possibilities that appear relevant to the problem. The artist, in his willingness to take chances, accepts the possibility of failure as part of his work. The artist, willing to operate in this manner, approaches the art process as an adventure and is seldom satisfied with the obvious and immediate solutions. School art often lacks the above qualities. Children should not be presented with an oversimplified version, polished steps, and defined end products leading to immediate and easily identifiable success. All frustrations and risks or the actual possibility of "failure" should not be avoided for students. Art experience in the school has to explore some sense of the struggle and tension that enter into the artist's exploring the unknown. Great satisfactions cannot exist without conquering uncertainties. Artists often feel that they don't always know all the answers or all the possible solutions in their investigation. They, however, share the understanding that their attempts, often only learning experiences, build knowledge that may be referred to at a later point. Art teaching has to aware children that as in other areas of study, art requires periods of learning, skill formations, and initial struggle before mastery. Children who would not expect to play an instrument or master a complicated math problem often are quick to judge their success and art abilities (lack of success). Art teaching has to clarify for the child what he feels he knows in reality (i.e., knowing what the face looks like is not the same knowledge as being able to reconstruct it on paper). The child who can see a tree and knows what it looks like is often turned off to art when he finds he cannot represent it on paper. The artist believes that time is an important factor in art making and art viewing. To be able to see, understand, and formulate visual statements, time must be afforded. The visual process cannot be rushed. School training often leads to quick visual comprehensions in reading, quick recall and recognition on exams, and quick understanding of complex ideas broken down into easily understandable curriculum steps.

The artist expresses a sense of seriousness about his work. School art often treats the subject as an area for recreation and relaxation. The seriousness of purposes will come through introducing the artist as a realistic concept.

Artistic Inspiration. The study of the artist must consider how the artist selects his ideas. The artist is above all curious and concerned with all visual phenomena. He is an avid observer and recorder. Simple experiences for environmental observations and recordings may be made in school including sketchbooks, visual idea files, rubbings, and photographs. The artist, based on his observations, develops visual systems or tentative solutions. The artist is a collector of visual ideas of other artists, art workings, and objects in general. His collections form the basis for his own creative arrangements and ideas. The artist is also a collector of new material and an experimenter with techniques and processes. Material and process experiments are useful tools in opening up creative ideas in the school. Less controlled processes including those of chance and fantasy are rich sources for inspiration. For the artist it is often a combination of visual and physical experiences with the reliance on chance and fantasy and the combination of both on which works are based. In observing art classes, one often hears the teacher give directions and then direct the class "to be creative." Creative ideas may be provided through visual inspirations derived only from space, environment, material, and processes.

The artist works with formal problems of design, exploring unlimited combinations of colors, specific lights, textures, spaces, balances, etc. Individual experiments based on problems of design may be sources of ideas. Other artists may be indirectly challenged through problems defined by their clients. Part of the inspiration comes from clients' stated problem and needs, followed by visual brainstorming. The art teacher may direct specific problems with limited boundaries which the students may expand upon.

Contemporary artists often use a combination of media and experiments for ideas and resources. Artistic inspirations seldom can be traced to a single source. Planning has to consider a variety of the above areas for investigation.

The Knowledge and Skills of the Artist. The artist possesses a unique array of skills and knowledges that prepare him for his work. Often these are not the skills and knowledges taken up by school art programs.

The artist understands the fundamental concerns of art and is able to construct problems and experiments to research them. The artist in the school is to understand that art is concerned in the development of visual statements through the exploration of color, line, shape, texture, and movement. Children may come to view the artist as a composer of these visual elements. School art may stress the concern in the study of art elements, their relationships, and various applications in use.

The artist is a visually perceptive individual who is able to see and select from varied aspects of the environment ideas of interest. He is able to combine his selection into a personal statement. Art teaching has to follow similar exposures.

The artist has developed his critical skills to enable him to sort out his own best ideas from both the environment and his work. Art education has to include the development of critical skills, i.e., to be able to criticize one's work, to view one's own work critically in relation to other works.

The artist's knowledge of history and current contemporary concerns of art is essential to his work. The work of the artist is often a rejection or an extension of ideas exposed by other artists. For the student who will use contemporary art as a basis for study, he must be exposed to the history of art. Since the art world is complex and involved, its study cannot be relegated until secondary school art appreciation courses.

The artist understands the process of research. He is able to identify a need, search out possible solution ideas, introduce relevant resources. He is able to expand upon ideas and formulate insights. The art problem is to teach children to use visual tools and processes to conduct experiments designed by both the teacher and student.

Artistic skill is knowing how to begin a problem; to take an idea and put it into action. The artist also knows when to stop or conclude a work. Both are major decision points. In the school art program, problems are too often defined by the teacher and their conclusion decided upon by the clock. In order to prepare students for independent actions, these two decision points should be made progressively more independently.

The artist does not copy from the environment. He selects elements of interest and makes significant changes. This free use of visual resources can be applied to art teaching. Projects dealing with artistic selection may be followed by exercises in simplification, enlargement, or abstraction of what is seen. Children may exercise changes by focusing in on details, reversing color schemes, and filtering visual information in a variety of ways. The artist's awareness of his work permits him to conclude major interests and directions which the work should stress. One's own artwork is often the best clue and model for other artworks. School art problems are often considered only in terms of teachers' directions and concern. Art teaching can be helpful in allowing students to work out ideas in a series or by using one artwork as the model for another, continuously allowing students to evaluate their work and decide on future directions. Art workings may focus on favorite colors, processes, themes, or shapes to be studied in depth.

The artist has creative intelligence, the ability to generate a problem, and the capability to gather resources and to experimentally find the most effective resources. The artist is able to stop at various stages of work and step back, evaluate, rethink, and return with additional insights.

The art teacher has to design the art experience so to allow the student to sort out his ideas to continuously clarify in removing things that are unnecessary and/or add details that will strengthen the visual statement.

CHOOSING ARTISTIC MODELS

The artist is a specialist in his particular area. The future art teacher should develop a speciality and at the same time should pose as a number of different visual artists. The study of the artist must include an example of the similarities and differences in materials, tools, space arrangements, client relationship, art workings, and trends in all the visual arts. Models may be based on the fashion designer, the architect, industrial designer, photographer, interior designer, advertising artist, sculptor, etc. Art training for future art teachers is to include introducing experiences in each of these fields.

Traditional art programs in the school have been defined in terms of painting and drawing, using the fine arts as a basis. This is not unusual, considering that art teachers on most levels come from a fine arts background. It is important to note, however, that the career interest and career development of all artists start early in life and should be encouraged at an early stage. A child who plays in the sandbox is not far removed from the adult architect. A child who makes paper clothing, or who arranges furniture in a doll house, is not far removed from the adult decorator. Early encouragement, exposures, and skill learnings help to form career awareness and interest.

To develop an art program based around the various artistic models, teaching may focus on the environment where all the visual arts are represented. The examination of similarities between the arts may use the study of design as its common point of reference since all artists deal with shapes, colors, and textures. Experiments may be developed to illustrate the similarities.

The teacher should strive to provide as realistic a model for student experiences as possible. Problems should be suggested which are appropriate to a particular artist. Tools, materials, and techniques could be a means of sampling each profession. The classroom environment may be altered to simulate the work space used by the artist. Specific room setups should consider the different types of surfaces, scales, physical positions, movements that are common to each. Each of the arts has unique means of recording visual information and processing it into a finished product. Part of the experience should be the linking of the child to the artist, including familiarity with examples of his product and comparisons with the child's own work. The following is a list of suggested experiences that may be used to characterize the illustrated artist. Suggestions may form the basis for individual project decisions.

The Fashion Designer. Experiences in fabric design including printing, dying, stenciling, and batiking. Experiences in comparing materials in different textures, weights, colors. Experiences in design including sketches for garments, two-dimensional paper constructions, simple drapings, use of special tools including tracing wheels, pins, needles, thread, pinking shears. Experiences in the design process should include fabric selection, learning about patterns, and constructing simple garments. References to the fashion world including exposures to contemporary fashion, should include magazines and visuals. Connections should be formed between other art forms including concepts of the figure as it's handled by the sculptor and the fashion photographer.

The Architect. Experiences in working with forms beginning with geometric plans, volumes, and blocks in a grid arrangement and in an open format. Experiences with space designs in forming divisions, partitions on a small scale, modular forms, working out space divisions in the artroom itself. The study of experimental building designs making block houses, designing caves, tree homes, tents, and trailers.

Observation and recordings of building details including the study of doors, stairs, roofs, etc. Experiencing the architectural process by making sketches, floor plans, elevations, and three-dimensional models. Study of architectural examples, different materials used, various ways buildings are constructed, and the study of architecture in relation to other contemporary arts, including minimal sculpture and monumental painting.

The Industrial Designer. Experiences in analyzing industrially-designed items familiar to the child including toys, packaging, and simple machinery. Experiences in considering the relationships between forms and their function using familiar objects including chairs or chewing gum. Discuss the reasons for material shape and color decisions by the artist. Experiencing the design process, working from sketches to cardboard prototypes for machine production, making simple molds and casts. Collection and comparison of different materials used in contemporary design. Developing one's own designs according to specifications by the teacher including initial criticism and refinement.

The Photographer. Exploring the element of light using the light box, transparencies, photographs, and shadow boxes. Exploring the same object from a variety of angles, distances, and viewpoints. Taking photographs in a series of candid subjects and prearranged compositions. Experiences in lighting objects in different ways; passing light through objects, creating a light show. The study of photographs in advertising, fine arts, reporting, and film.

The Interior Designer. Exploring familiar interiors and items in the home. Selection and comparison on a single familiar object such as a chair. Experiences in the design process, taking measurements, making templates, sketch of an existing space, create a model that can be manipulated, create a mood and environment in the artroom space. Experiences in comparing interiors including business and private spaces. Experiments in composing color schemes, lighting arrangements, and form arrangements. Using existing chairs or pieces of furniture, experiment in redesigning given forms. Experiences in working for a client (teacher), solving a problem by involving the client in the decision-making process. Plan a presentation of an idea to a client.

The Advertising Artist. Explore the various forms of advertising including magazines, billboards, logos, packaging. Experiences in advertising including the writing of slogans (or copy) using photographs, cartoons, or illustrations to depict a story idea. Experiments with specific advertising techniques such as the use of repetition of images, exaggeration, removing lettering from its context, and simplification of messages. Processes in advertising including page layout, type selection, photography experiences in creating visual impact using color choices, color arrangements, symmetry, repetition, and scale.

The Sculptor. Experiences may be based on the study of the figure, its shapes, and movements. Experiences may include the building of armatures (skeletal system) and various material coverings (skin). Experiments may include contemporary sculptural items based on geometric and architectural forms and the assembly and arrangement of these forms. Sculpture experiences may include negative processes such as carving, or additive processes including the combination of ready-made objects and forms. Sculpture products may include relief work (plaster, sand casting) or contrasting works in the round. Reliefs may be explored in various depth under different lighting conditions. Sculpture experiences may include working with new and less permanent materials and processes such as plastics (inflatables), cardboard (wrapping), and rubber (stuffing) as techniques in making sculpture. Experiments in scale may include planning pieces for indoors to affect the artroom space or for outdoors to affect the environment. Sculpture experiences may include movements (either self-propelled, wind- or water-propelled, and simple machine-operated).

THE LANGUAGE OF THE ARTIST

The artist has a refined and a developed sense of vision. He is able to receive, interpret, and formulate visual messages. The artist's language is based on his observation and manipulation of color, light, line, form, shape, and texture. At present, most school communication is through verbal, not visual channels. Art teaching itself is often verbal using visual aids to illustrate verbal statements. Elementary school art suffers from this verbal emphasis as children are inclined to concentrate on stories and verbalize through the artworks they produce.

Artist's Communications. Future art teachers should recognize similarities between the artist structuring the environment of his canvas and the art teacher's structuring his lesson. As the artist communicates through his selection of materials, spaces, and environment in preparing for work, the art teacher has to make similar preparations. (See p. 93.)

The artist communicates his ability and interest in art in his contact with materials; in the way he holds, carries, and manipulates equipment and materials. He displays confidence and mastery. The way he sets up the art experience for others communicates his own interest and involvement in art. Examples of the teacher's artwork or the teacher's selection of the works of others define his interest, tastes, and concerns. Artworks brought into class have to be considered as powerful communicators. Examples should not only be carefully selected but preferably grouped to express various possibilities.

Each art profession has unique communication and media possibilities. To study how various artists communicate may be an appropriate area of investigation. Comparisons of communication, for example, may consider the different messages of newspaper ads, spot commercials, a painting, or an interior of a bank.

Artists are often able to communicate in several media. Painters, for example, may prepare drawings or sketches for their work, may produce photographs or sculptural forms based on an idea. The elementary school child may explore simple messages worked through various art media. Exploration may include using one media as a model for another.

The artist communicates through his work a position or attitude regarding the art world. Art teachers in the selection of projects exemplify a personal aesthete. Although one's own art base and experience is an excellent place to start, art teachers are called upon to teach a wider range of art concerns than their own. Art communication which appears to be intuitive is, in fact, controllable and manageable if one is aware of one's own taste and preferences. It is expressed in one's selection of problems, use of models, materials, and arrangement of the art room space.

The Artist as a Performer. All artistic actions involve performances. The art performances are recorded in the work. The observance of the performance in action may be as instructive as the product. The performance in a sense separates the layers of the finished product for close consideration (see p. 75). The traditional forms of art teaching which rely on lecture remove the teacher from artistic performance. Art teaching has taken place in two independent sequences: the first, in which the art teacher demonstrates (seldom visual performances) and the students become a passive audience deriving direction from the demonstration; and the second, a reversal of the first. That is, the students work while the teacher becomes an observer. In an art program based on an artistic model, there would not exist such a clear separation. Active participation and communication through art would be continuous during the lesson. The teacher as well as the student would perform and communicate visually. Learning this process involves discontinuing the lecture from the front of the room, not considering teaching as lecturing in front of an audience, and structuring one's lesson as a visual performance instead of a demonstration. It also involves the preparation for the scene of communication (see p. 101) before the children enter the art room. The teacher may, through his work, invite participation, react, and criticize work through visual means (sketches, tracings, diagrams, illustrations).

Children must see the art teacher not as the lecturer or verbal communicator but a visual planner and performer, and the art process as an intermediary or a source of communication.

The Special Nature of Art Communication. The artist's communication is a combination of personal expression and the communication of ideas to others. In viewing artist's works, the child should be discouraged from only looking for verbal or story content since the artist is sending visual messages and not abstractions of a story or subject. The artist does not write or tell stories in paint. He is principally concerned to structure communication through line, color, and shape into visual statements. The art teacher should discourage cliches such as "you are to see in an artwork what you feel—not what the artist expresses." Since artists are communicating, it is extremely important to understand what it is they are communicating. Understanding, however, is the visual process of seeing and not a literary guessing. Understanding has to come in terms of how the artist has combined his visual alphabet.

THE ARTIST IN THE CLASSROOM

To teach art, one must have the confidence to engage in art working in front of the class and with the students. It means having personally experienced some of the elements of each lesson and deriving understanding as well as motivation from one's own experiences. The artist in the classroom should not merely repeat the art lessons that others have developed. They must rework and reformulate lessons and thus become experts on the problem before teaching it to others. A projection of one's creative self has to be consciously planned as a significant element in one's teaching.

Striving to Become the Artist in the Class. The art teacher may project himself as a creative individual by accepting and encouraging a variety of solution ideas. In school, children often strive to finish a work as fast as possible because they have been trained that reward comes at the end. The art teacher must continuously praise diverse solutions throughout the work and stress the satisfaction of the process of art making. The teacher must plan lessons openly to suggest many possible directions. Lessons should be planned visually through drawings, diagrams, and sketches. He must share his own collections of artworks and objects and his experiences in visiting galleries and museums. In raising oneself to the status of the artist in the class, one encourages the artistic strivings of others.

Children learn instinctively as to what is considered important in their school program. Their attitude formation is directly related to the attitudes of the teacher. Having an involved artist in the class is the most effective way to serve as a source of interest and identification for the child's future commitment (to art). The artistic setting also creates an atmosphere where all personal ideas, inventions, and innovations are welcome.

Planning Your Role as the Artist in the Class. The environment in the room should be kept flexible and open. All surfaces should be considered as possibilities for art works. The environment is to be set up according to the art experience being prepared and the visual artist emphasized. The space should provide interest with the introduction of outside objects. The art room should be considered as one of the bases of motivations and inspiration for art problems. Innovative approaches to exhibiting artworks outside of the class should be sought in gallery and museum exhibits.

One should not be restricted to typical bulletin board frames. Possibilities should include one-man shows, teacher and student exhibitions, murals and special exhibitions of found objects. The artist's experience of seeing one's work in an exhibit is an appropriate experience for school children. Based on his exhibit, the artist should be encouraged to describe his feelings, ideas, and possible future directions for his work. The teacher must plan and evaluate lessons visually; to *show* as much as he tells, *perform* as much as he lectures.

One should encourage the total art interests of the students. Encouragement should be given to continuously work outside of the school to record and plan visual ideas. The teacher should be continuously willing to share and respond to art works of students. One of the ways to express importance is by giving art an equal time consideration with other subjects and a prime time for the art lesson.

The art teacher does not have to feel that he has to be prepared with all the answers. Art teaching should be viewed as a matter of providing the opportunity for students to search out their own solutions. Teachers do not have to feel that they have all the skills and techniques. To teach skills is meaningless without inspiring individual ideas. Having ideas, the child will develop many of the necessary skills for his art statement.

ART IN SPECIAL EDUCATION

The Blind. The ability of senses to substitute for each other forms the basis of art education attempting to develop all other senses of the blind. Opportunity may be provided to widen their sensory capability and help them interpret their experience. Art activities can help blind children recall direction and the extent of children's movement. Through feeling art objects they can begin to build permanent mental pictures for themselves. Manipulative art workings may include 3D objects such as wood blocks or pegboards. Other material such as plaster or clay may be molded and and left to harden enabling pupils to retrace hand movements at a future time. It is useful to define the space in which the child is to work to use a box so that the child feels the boundaries of material and activity.

Brain Injured. Brain damage leaves a child with uncoordinated movement, sometimes appearing to lack a natural feeling for rhythm. Such children may have incomplete knowledge of body image and a lack of sense of direction and distance. These children may use art to develop maximum hand and finger movements through activities involving the feel of shapes and materials. In this process they gain mental stimulus from movement as well as improved muscular coordination. The development of purposeful movement, through art using repetitive performance, helps in improving a sense of relationships. Art activities, based on simple sensory experiences, should be readily repeated by these children for the pure physical pleasure as well as tangible results. A hand which, through art, becomes useful to the child, is more relaxed and normal in movement. Repetition is an essential part of art therapy (providing interesting patterns in the movements, as well as essential memories recorded in these movements).

Most activities for the special child may begin at the level of pleasant sensations. It is important to center art activity about the child's special needs, need for direct contact with materials and sensations, and of movement through the use of a variety of tools. There is a need for efforts to develop the lost senses of the deaf and the blind in the art experience—as well as to compensate for some of the physical problems of the handicapped. Appropriate rooms should be provided for the various physical movements to be encouraged (although many of the movements planned for in the art activity will be extensions of the movements the child already has). All art

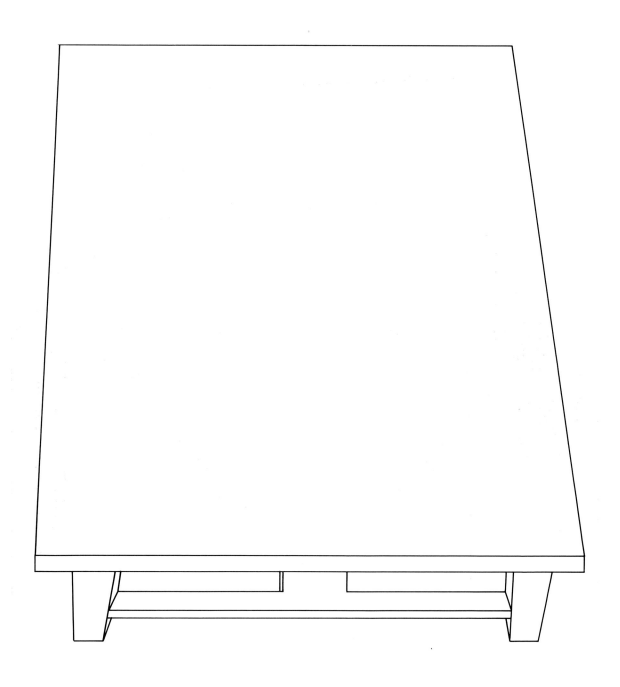

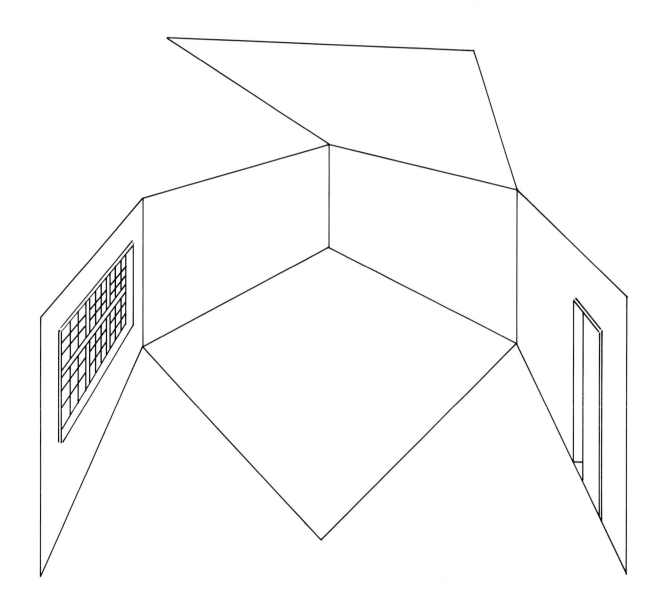

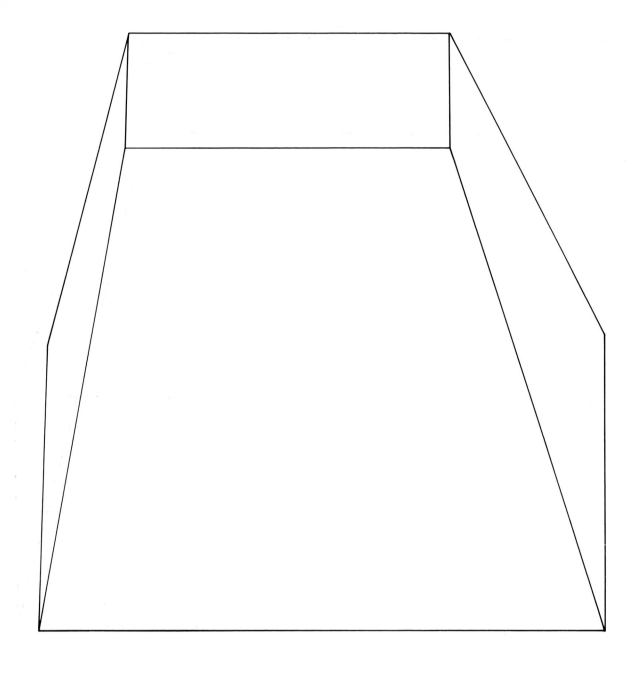

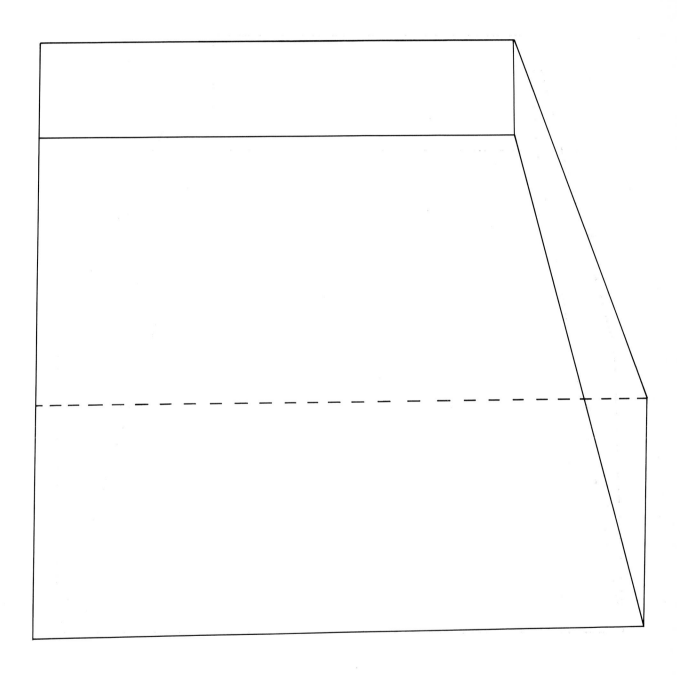

materials must be prepared for by the teacher in advance. Frustration should be kept to a minimum and self-achievement emphasized.

Students with Hearing Difficulties. Art can be particularly important to students who are deaf, or who have suffered a hearing loss—just as music can be especially meaningful to those who are blind or disabled. All creative movements can be explored, whether verbally (through written directions or sign language), or through nonverbal cues. Students can imitate, trace, improvise spontaneously with or without the teacher, plan designs, creatively structure a room or another environment, make pottery, or sculpt. (See pp 97-98 for other ideas).

Great composers who went deaf (such as Beethoven and Smetana) can serve as a source of inspiration. Students can learn how to draw music; they can even compose music if tones or tonal combinations are wired to particular lights in different colors. (Organs that emit different colored lights are commercially available.) Compositions created according to the aesthetic qualities of the color combinations can be "evaluated" by the teacher or students who can hear (not judged good or bad, of course, but evaluated in the sense of depicting and reflecting certain types of moods).

If certain types of perceptions, and senses of touch or smell, begin to compensate for the hearing loss, the perceptions and senses can be employed to help solve artistic problems. Thus, visual and tactile solutions to art problems might be quite different (if not superior)—in some ways, perhaps, superior to solutions conceived by those blessed with perfect hearing. We see then that if art is used in full measure with special education classes—even if out of a sense of fairness to those who are at this disadvantage—not only is their aesthetic sensitivity developed but society at large can be the beneficiary!

EPILOGUE

The multiplicity of sights, smells, and sounds of the city can be a source of great inspiration—as well as confusion and difficulty. The same students who manifest the most difficult behavioral problems can often generate the most excitement, whether in creative color combinations or rhythmic drumming. We have hoped that many of the ideas presented in this book are a beginning rather than an end; that future teachers will come up with new ideas for using cassette tape recorders; that future teachers will come up with new ideas for nonverbal communication channels; that future teachers will explore new ways of combining music and art with a bilingual program; that future teachers will not exclude art or music from the special education curriculum; and that art and music will continue to flourish and thrive in our great urban centers.

bibliography

Art Education

Alschuler, Rose H., and Hattwick, La Berta W. *Painting and Personality.* Chicago: University of Chicago Press, 1947.

Art Education: Elementary. Washington, D.C.: National Art Education Association, 1972.

Axline, Virginia M. *Play Therapy.* New York: Random House, 1969.

Battcock, Gregory. *New Ideas in Art Education.* New York: E.P. Dutton and Co., Inc., 1973.

——. *The New Art.* New York: E.P. Dutton and Co., Inc., 1966.

Bland, Jane C. *Art of the Young Child.* Greenwich, Conn.: New York Graphic Society, 1968.

Borreson, Mary J. *Let's Go to an Art Museum.* New York: G.P. Putnam's Sons, 1960.

Canaday, John. *Mainstreams of Modern Art: David to Picasso.* New York: Simon and Schuster, 1959.

Coen, K., and Coen, G. *Musical Instruments in Art.* Minneapolis, Minn.: Lerner Publications Co., 1965.

Conrad, George. *The Process of Art Education in the Elementary School.* Englewood Cliffs, N.J.: Prentice-Hall, Inc., 1964.

Cornelius, Chase, and Cornelius, Sue. *The City in Art.* Minneapolis, Minn.: Lerner Publications Co., 1965.

Dover, Cedric. *American Negro Art.* Greenwich, Conn.: New York Graphic Society, 1969.

Downer, Marion. *Children in the World's Art.* New York: Lothrop, Lee and Shepard Co., Inc., 1970.

Eisner, Elliott W. *Education Artistic Vision.* New York: Macmillan Co., 1972.

Feldman, Edmund Burke. *Becoming Human Through Art: Aesthetic Experience in the School.* Englewood Cliffs, N.J.: Prentice-Hall, Inc., 1970.

Gaitskell, Charles D., and Hurwitz, Al. *Children and Their Art.* 2nd ed. New York: Harcourt, Brace and World, Inc., 1970.

Gregor, Arthur S. *How the World's Cities Began.* New York: E.P. Dutton and Co., Inc., 1972.

Hall, Edward T. *The Silent Language.* Garden City, N.Y.: Anchor Press, 1973.

Hart, Tony. *The Young Designer.* New York: Frederick Warne & Co., Inc., 1968.

Hartley, Ruth E., and Goldenson, Robert M. *The Complete Book of Children's Play.* New York: Thomas Y. Crowell Company, 1963.

Herberholz, Donald, and Herberholz, Barbara. *A Child's Pursuit of Art.* Dubuque, Ia.: Wm. C. Brown Company Publishers, 1967.

Jameson, Kenneth. *Art and the Young Child.* New York Viking Press, 1970.

Kohn, Bernice. *Everything Has a Shape and Everything Has a Size.* Englewood Cliffs, N.J.: Prentice-Hall, Inc., 1964.

Lark-Horovitz, Betty; Lewis, Hilda; and Luca, Mark. *Understanding Children's Art for Better Teaching.* Columbus, Ohio: Charles E. Merrill Books, Inc., 1967.

Laury, Jean R., and Aiken, Joyce. *Creative Body Coverings.* New York: Van Nostrand Reinhold Company, 1973.

Lewis, Hilda P., ed. *Art for the Preprimary Child.* Washington, D.C.: National Art Education Association, 1972.

Linderman, Marlene. *Art in the Elementary School: Drawing, Painting, and Creating for the Classroom.* Dubuque, Ia.: Wm. C. Brown Company Publishers, 1974.

Lowenfeld, Viktor. *Your Child and His Art.* New York: Macmillan Co., 1965.

Marzollo, Jean, and Trivas, Irene. *Learning Through Play.* New York: Harper & Row, Publishers, 1972.

Pickering, John M. *Visual Education in the Primary School.* New York: Watson-Guptill Publications, 1971.

Robbin, Irving. *The How and Why Book of Caves to Skyscrapers.* New York: Wonder Books, 1963.

Schwartz, Alvin. *Old Cities and New Towns: The Changing Face of the Nation.* New York: E.P. Dutton and Co., Inc., 1968.

Sherwood, Ruth F. *Homes Today and Tomorrow.* Peoria, Illinois: Chas. A. Bennett Co., Inc., 1972.

Wolf, Thomas H. *The Magic of Color.* New York: Odyssey Press, 1964.

Music Education

Adler, Marvin S. *Developing Understanding of Twentieth Century Compositions in Junior High School General Music Classes.* Ann Arbor: University Microfilms International, 1971. Order #71-1088 (contains many additional references on musical styles, trends, and media.)

Apel, Willi, and Daniel, Ralph T. (eds.) *The Harvard Brief Dictionary of Music.* New York: Washington Square Press, 1966.

Berger, Donald Paul. *Folk Songs of Japanese Children.* Tokyo: Charles E. Tuttle Co., 1969.

Bruner, Jerome S. *The Process of Education.* New York: Vintage Books, 1960.

Eisman, Lawrence; Jones, Elizabeth; and Malone, Raymond. *Making Music Your Own.* Morristown: Silver Burdett Company, 1971.

Machlis, Joseph. *The Enjoyment of Music.* New York: W.W. Norton and Co., 1970.

Tipton, Gladys. *Adventures in Music.* New York: R.C.A. Victor.

Ulrich, Homer. *Music a Design for Listening.* New York: Harcourt, Brace and World Inc., 1959.

Winslow, Robert, and Dallin, Leon. *Music Skills for Classroom Teachers.* Dubuque, Ia.: Wm. C. Brown Company Publishers, 1971.

music index

song index

c = complete

art index